THE
HALLMAN
LEGACY

IMPACT OF THE HALLMAN FAMILY
IN WATERLOO REGION

John G. Fast

◆ FriesenPress

One Printers Way
Altona, MB R0G 0B0
Canada

www.friesenpress.com

ISBN
978-1-03-914390-6 (Hardcover)
978-1-03-914389-0 (Paperback)
978-1-03-914391-3 (eBook)

1. BIOGRAPHY & AUTOBIOGRAPHY, BUSINESS

Distributed to the trade by The Ingram Book Company

ADVANCED PRAISE FOR:

THE HALLMAN LEGACY: IMPACT OF THE HALLMAN FAMILY IN WATERLOO REGION.

JOHN G. FAST

Everyone's heard the term "family business" but not all fully grasp the unique challenges this corporate hybrid poses. Here's a fascinating look at an ultra-successful family business that transformed its local landscape through construction and the long-term care sector. It's a business book but also an analysis of complex family dynamics and how philanthropy can be a lengthening shadow of personal values. Although one might not be surprised by the inherent complexity of these dynamics, what might raise appreciative eyebrows is the book's uncommon candor. "How," readers may wonder, "did they let the author say this?" It's a few-holds-barred story showing powerful personalities of common kinship striving together to meet community needs and bolster local initiatives.

You'll see how the Hallman clan's robust entrepreneurship joined hands with compassionate stewardship to build one of Canada's largest philanthropic trusts. The result has empowered more than a hundred organizations serving critical social, educational and mental health needs of children and families.

Along the way are insights galore, with crosscutting themes interacting in fascinating ways – cars, construction, sports, land development and eldercare, to name a few.

—**Wally Kroeker**, *retired editor of The Marketplace magazine*

What a thoroughly enjoyable read. And what a gift – not only to the Hallman family but to those of us working in family businesses who are awed both by the incredible achievements over a lifetime and the example of perseverance through some incredible complex, if not only too human family dynamics.

—**family business member**

What a precious treasure John Fast and Jim Hallman have given to the Region of Waterloo and beyond. *The Hallman Legacy* captures the complexities of how one family has shaped so much of the success and quality of life in Waterloo Region. This is a story of real people with courageous vision, power and wealth who have never lost their humility or their commitment to social good and service to others. It is a must-read epic love story of the Hallman's and their community.

—**Cathy Brothers**, *CEO of Capacity Canada*

The Hallman Legacy succeeds wonderfully in conveying the exceptional legacy of the family while explaining how the business succeeded so well in Waterloo Region. A region that was transformed by the housing Lyle and his family built. The book provides an excellent portrait of Jim, describing how he has done a wonderful job of making a good thing, the Foundation, a great institution.

—**John English**, *former MP, official biographer of Lester Pearson and award winning biographer of Pierre Trudeau; Distinguished University Professor Emeritus, University of Waterloo*

This captivating saga weaves a historical account that is better than fiction. The candid expose includes challenging personalities, turbulent relationships, and gripping tragedies. Through three generations, beginning with Grandfather Anson, the Hallman family has displayed a near immutable "DNA" that champions integrity, diligence, discipline, frugality, and self-sacrifice. An abiding mantra is – keep doing better. Almost mystically, one encounters an alchemy in which the customary trapping of family fortune is converted into the remarkable Lyle S. Hallman Foundation with its astounding financial assets and noble pursuits. Its far-reaching, Waterloo Region impact, embraces transformative support of higher education and health care, rescuing disenfranchised, needy individuals, and promoting organizations that instil a vision of hope within the community.

This story offers a real-world case study that will undoubtedly be dissected in fields of psychology, sociology, and business management. Hopefully, though, the template of this legacy will be indelibly imprinted upon successive Hallman generations to – "Earn all you can, save all you can, and give all you can." (John Wesley).

—**Jake J. Thiessen, Ph.D.** *First Hallman Director,*
School of Pharmacy, University of Waterloo

All history is personal. And *The Hallman Legacy* is personal to all who live in Waterloo Region. *The Hallman Legacy* describes the values and commitment of four generations of the Hallman family with all of the complex passions, tragedies, struggles, and commitments that come to define their lives. To read this account as outlined by John Fast is to be overwhelmed by how the Hallman's sense of community and civic values shaped their concerns for improving the community in ways that few of us could ever have realized. Like the Hallman legacy, this is a book that will stand the test of time and enrich those who read it.

—**Kenneth McLaughlin**, *author,*
Distinguished Professor Emeritus, University of Waterloo

I am delighted to see this important memoir of the Hallmans. They were such key leaders and builders in the Waterloo region and set such an inspiring example for so many others during a crucial time as Waterloo was emerging as Canada's leader in innovation. One story illustrates this observation. I had just arrived in Waterloo to join the University. Lyle had just made the largest gift the University had ever received. It was $2 million. His focus was on health and promoting healthy living. From those discussions came the Lyle Hallman Health Centre in our Faculty of Applied Health Sciences. The Faculty was on the cusp of take off and with this gift over the next decade, it simply flourished. But Lyle's leadership also inspired the entire University. Its custom since its founding was to run a major capital campaign once every decade. During the campaigns of the two previous decades the University raised approximately $60 million. During the campaign for the first decade from the year 2000 with Lyle's gift as a foundation stone the University raised 11 times that amount - over $660 million. The University never looked back; nor did the Waterloo region. Thus, are great institutions and great communities built. Great leaders make a difference. Lyle was one of these giants.

—**The Right Honourable David Johnston**,
28th Governor General of Canada (2010 to 2017)

This book on the Hallman Legacy provides a strong narrative together with absorbingly interesting details that provide very good insight about the family dynamics. I found the book honest and accurate while also being sympathetic to the complexity of their story.

—**Karen Redman**, *Regional Chair, Waterloo Region*

Table of Contents

FOREWORD

This project started, as most do, with a simple thought. I wanted to honour what would have been my father's 100th birthday and celebrate 75 years of Hallman Construction, which gave birth to the Lyle S. Hallman Foundation. This simple thought grew into a book proposal. My original goal for this book was to commemorate the 100-plus years of our Hallman family in business—recount our humble beginnings, the hardships and trials along the way, and end up where we are today: a large, fully functioning granting foundation. I wanted to show the impact of our work.

This book in front of you is the final result. But as you'll see, it doesn't chronicle one singular journey—our legacy is the result of an amazing collaborative effort.

As I thought about our lives and remembered past events, I discovered a tale of not only how we grew, but how we succeeded in spite of how we grew. My father, Lyle, was a trail-blazing figure in Canadian history throughout the twentieth century. He would have hit the century mark in 2022. He was clearly someone who made a tremendous contribution to his home community, Waterloo Region, as both a businessman and a philanthropist. But he wasn't an easy man. He was a colourful actor, a strong, often difficult personality. We were also not a meek family. Our story reads more like a family-business melodrama than a dry-bones history. It includes tragic events and moments of family tenderness, strategic business decisions, and monumental civic leadership. Lives are changed. Lives are lost. Fortunes are made. Wealth is dispersed. Families unite. Families separate.

Yet, I believe this book captures how we, as Hallmans, have done well and also how we continue to do good. Doing well and doing good don't always come in the same package. But when they do, it usually makes for an interesting story.

In this book, you'll read about the lives and contributions of my father, Lyle, and his children, with a focus on two of his sons: Peter Hallman and, me, Jim Hallman. Despite (or because of) our relationship dynamics and propelled by our unique leadership strengths, we built one of the largest property development companies in South Central Ontario. We also created one of Canada's largest public trusts. The Lyle S. Hallman Foundation has contributed almost $90 million to Waterloo Region's social, educational, and mental health services since 2004. And we're on track to grant more than $15 million annually to Waterloo Region for decades to come.

To me, the Hallman legacy means so much more than business success and financial largesse. I hope that our examples of civic leadership and community service inspire you to join the drive to contribute to the greater common good.

Jim Hallman
President, Hallman Construction
Chair, Lyle S. Hallman Foundation

At its core, the Hallman legacy is about civic leadership and community service.

Right: Lyle S. Hallman Institute For Health Promotion at the University of Waterloo

Bottom left: Lyle S. Hallman Faculty of Social Work at Wilfrid Laurier University

Bottom right: Lyle Hallman Pool at Grand River Recreation Complex

PREFACE

I have had the privilege of being both Jim Hallman's and Peter Hallman's friend. My first encounter with Jim was playing hockey in the early 1990s. I was a substitute player on an established senior men's team when he passed the puck to me and I missed a good scoring opportunity.

He skated up to me with a big smile on his face and laughingly said, "I see you like cherry-picking… but if you keep your stick on the ice, you might actually score some goals."

My first significant interaction with Peter occurred in the mid-1990s. We met during a learning event on the topic of family business succession. I had invited Peter to participate on the panel, and as he left that meeting, he turned to me and said, "Let's have lunch tomorrow. We've got much more to discuss." Peter was not going to let moss grow on that topic.

These early encounters were the start of a twenty-five-year journey of walking alongside the extended Hallman family. Our circle of friendship includes their sister, Susan, and her children, Kevin, Brian, and Kaitlyn; Peter's wife, Brenda, and their sons, Brent, Greg, and Mark; and Jim's wife, Sue, and their children, Nathan and Kerri. I feel honoured to have been invited into some of their most sacred spaces and meaningful moments.

Having a front row seat to the family's story is not necessarily a qualification for writing this book, and I also do not claim impartiality. However, it does give me a unique insight into this family's journey and their all-too-human attempts to balance love, money, and power.

In our early conversations about the book proposal, we realized that thirty years had passed since the *Lyle S. Hallman Story* was published in 1992. We also recognized that the Hallman impact was far more complex than one individual family's story. Until the time of Lyle's death in 2003, the Hallman story was of a multi-generational family business. Although it is no longer a family business story, the impact of this family continues.

The writing of this book included more than sixty interviews with people who helped shape or were shaped by the Hallmans' impact. Their experiences, stories, and insights helped me tell this story. And the story continues, as the Hallman Foundation is nearing its twentieth anniversary in 2023.

My front-row seat to the family's story includes my involvement in facilitating significant strategic moments in their various business ventures: Hallman Eldercare, Aberdeen Homes, Hallman Construction, and more recently, the Hallman Foundation. Those experiences helped inform the following pages, providing in-depth background and rich texture.

Another chapter in the Hallman story remains to be written. Twelve next-generation Hallmans are currently making significant contributions within their communities, and they are creating their own distinct legacy. There will be many more stories. And the Hallman impact will continue to endure.

John G. Fast, PhD
The Family Business Doctor

INTRODUCTION

I f you were visiting Waterloo Region for the first time, you would soon notice a significant Hallman presence. You might find yourself at a swim meet in the Lyle S. Hallman Pool. You might enroll at Wilfrid Laurier University's Lyle S. Hallman Faculty of Social Work or explore a degree program at the University of Waterloo's School of Public Health Sciences, which is housed in the Lyle S. Hallman Institute for Health Promotion. You might run into the Hallman Director of the School of Pharmacy at Canada's only co-op pharmacy program on U of W's downtown Kitchener campus. And if you were looking to purchase a house, you might find the Grand River South neighbourhood attractive because of Eden Oak Trail Park. Hallman Construction, which developed the subdivision, invested significant funds to create the adjacent park for nearby residents.

These are some of the family's more visible contributions to the region, but they don't begin to reflect the breadth and depth of the Hallman impact on their community. Hallman Construction began in 1946, and over the past 75 years, it has arguably developed the greatest amount of property within Waterloo Region. Until relatively recently, it had been one of the largest landlords in the area. This good news business story has evolved into a story about sharing. The Lyle S. Hallman Foundation has become one of Canada's largest philanthropic trusts, projected to donate over $15 million annually to Waterloo Region, to help over 100 organizations better serve the social, educational, and mental health needs of children and their families.

As leaders, the Hallmans have had to overcome difficulties, handle tragedies, and resolve conflicts. To be able to contribute to the wider community and obtain real, tangible results requires strategic leadership. It also requires a deep level of empathy.

Although this book is a story about the profound impact the Hallmans have made on Waterloo Region, their legacy is not well known or understood. When Jim Hallman received the 2018 Kiwanis Citizen of the Year Award for Kitchener in an event with the largest attendance on record, it became apparent that the Hallman contribution to the region was a somewhat well-kept secret. For many, it was the first time they had heard about the significant impact of the Lyle S. Hallman Foundation, though it is one of Canada's largest public trusts. Even close friends seemed surprised.

"I had no idea that you were involved in so many significant projects."

"We didn't even know what it is that you do."

For almost 200 years, members of the Hallman family have helped shape the prosperous Waterloo Region. Their legacy endures and is poised for significant contributions well into the future. Their story deserves to be celebrated and shared.

Lyle S. Hallman, introverted, philanthropic, analytical decision maker.
He saw himself as a founder responsible for doing everything.

Peter Hallman, dominant, charismatic, tireless consensus builder.
He redefined the Hallman impact through his multiple civic leadership roles
and dedicated community service.

Jim Hallman, independent, subtle, tenacious peacemaker. He emerged as the effective clean-up hitter, propelling the Hallman impact far into the future.

THE HALLMAN FAMILY

History shows it is never easy to navigate and manage the dynamics of business families. Love, money, and power, when attained, present predictable challenges. Those families that succeed in managing these dynamics have an incredible competitive advantage. And if they are both economically successful and able to nurture intergenerational harmony and goodwill, there is a particular sweetness in that.

The Hallmans, as with all business families, had to manage these difficult dynamics—especially the relationship between Lyle Hallman, Peter Hallman, and Jim Hallman—and the challenges of competing bottom lines. It remained a constant pressure as they tried to promote individual health and achieve family harmony.

But to understand these dynamics and this family properly, we have to go back to the beginning.

ORIGINAL SETTLERS

The first Hallman in North America was part of a wave of pioneers in Pennsylvania known as the *Pennsylvania Deitsch*. Anthony Hallman (or possibly Heilman) was born in Kleinniedesheim, Germany, in 1671 and moved to the German-speaking area around Philadelphia, in Skippack (originally spelled Skippach and named after a town in Bavaria). In 1720, he bought 150 acres of land for farming. Anthony was a churchwarden of the Lutheran Church at Trappe, Pennsylvania, but he was buried in the Mennonite graveyard adjacent to his farm. He had helped build the churchyard and been given permission to have a plot for his family. Some of his descendants followed suit, practising the Lutheran faith yet being buried in the Old Mennonite Cemetery next door.[1]

Anthony was also a strong character. In his will, for reasons he said he would not reveal, he disinherited his oldest son John, giving him only one English shilling. He gave his youngest son, Henry, the whole 150 acres and his household goods.[2]

Henry's grandson, Benjamin Hallman, Jr., suffered under the financial depression of the early nineteenth century. He sold his land, paid his debts, packed up two double-horse teams and one single-horse team, and moved up to Canada in 1825 where land was cheaper. He purchased 200 acres of mostly forested land about a mile outside of Roseville, North Dumfries Township, where he cleared land to build a beautiful farm.[3]

Roseville itself was about fourteen kilometres from Berlin, a settlement that was initially called Ebytown after the Mennonite preacher Benjamin Eby. It was named Berlin in the 1830s to reflect the townspeople's strong Germanic roots. In 1916, in the middle of World War I, Berlin was renamed Kitchener after a bitter name-changing debate to prove the residents' loyalty and stem anti-German backlash.[4]

Both towns lay within the Haldimand Tract, a long, thin tract of land that was granted to the Haudenosaunee of the Six Nations of the Grand River and is within the territory of the Neutral, Anishinaabe, and Haudenosaunee peoples.

Many of the immigrants to Canada between 1816 and the 1870s were German Lutherans and Swiss Mennonites. Although the original Hallman settler (Anthony) was Lutheran, the first Hallman settler in Canada (Benjamin, Jr.) was a member of the Mennonite Church. These two religious traditions, Lutheran and Mennonite, seemed to shape life-long impulses and motivations in the Hallman family throughout their heritage history. Integrity, hard work, and generosity were paramount virtues. Lyle learned them from his father, Anson, who learned them from his grandfather, Abraham, and so on. Lyle represented the ninth generation of Hallmans in North America, and the fifth generation to have settled in Ontario.[5]

Anson recalled that his grandfather, Abraham, "was a man of few words … loved by his neighbours and his own family. A neighbour told me how this was proved. Grandpa's cattle had gotten out on the road and into a neighbour's hayfield. The neighbour became very angry and began threatening him. When haying time came, Grandpa took a large load of hay to the neighbour and said, 'This is for the hay my cattle ate while they were in your field. Please take it and let's be neighbours again.' The neighbour then confessed that he left the gate open on purpose hoping to make a little money. Grandpa's action brought a profound respect."[6]

Anson also reflected these values. Lawyer Gerry Eastman remembers him as having "inherent goodness of the old type Mennonite! He didn't have to struggle to do right; to Anson, doing the right thing was the only way to go."

Lyle recalled his father as always being ethical. "We wouldn't ever sneak things across the border between the U.S. and Canada by saying we had nothing to declare."[7]

In the Hallman household, generosity was practised to a fault. Lyle's sister, Jean, recalled, "My parents gave, and gave, too much … And not just to us. They gave to others. One city mission worker told me—after he had preached a sermon—Dad came up to shake hands with him and left a one hundred dollar bill in the palm of his hand. That was when ten dollars was a lot of money."[8]

Anson Hallman's values originated from the Protestant work ethic (also known as the Calvinist work ethic or Puritan work ethic), which was preached and practised in most areas of his life. The Protestant work ethic emphasizes being diligent, disciplined, and frugal. A person's duty in life was to achieve success through hard work and thrift, and success would indicate a right and proper relationship with God.[9]

Earn all you can, save all you can, and give all you can.
Founder of Methodism John Wesley in "The Use of Money" sermon[10]

Lyle's Mennonite roots also shaped his personal life and business life. Mennonite beliefs emphasized hard work, integrity, collaboration, caring for the poor, and community-mindedness. His was a simple spirituality centred on following the practical example of Jesus in all aspects of one's daily life.

True evangelical faith cannot lie dormant,
It clothes the naked, it feeds the hungry,
It comforts the sorrowful, it shelters the destitute,
It serves those that harm it,
It binds up that which is wounded,
It has become all things to all creatures.
Menno Simons (founder of Anabaptism), 1539[11]

One very practical manifestation of this religious upbringing was tithing. Lyle's father always gave a tenth of his income to the church before anything else.[12] Lyle continued this practice of tithing throughout his life.

THE EARLY YEARS

Even as Lyle's character was shaped by the values of his family and faith, the economic situation of his family profoundly influenced his approach to work and future life decisions. After the stock market crashed in 1929, throwing the world into a global depression, Lyle's family began wrestling with bankruptcy and foreclosure. Anson owned a building supply store at the time, but a series of unfortunate blows—the almost complete stoppage of building compounded by a dishonest book-keeper—left them with debts totalling about $40,000, a substantial sum at the time. Although his father paid off his debts by 1943, the fear and trauma of living under a financial cloud and on the precipice of financial calamity took its toll.

As Lyle turned nine in 1931, Anson was informed that his family had one year to vacate the family home on the top of Shantz Hill just north of Preston—today the intersection of Highways 8 and 401 in Cambridge. For the lack of $3,000, Anson at age forty-five had to surrender the family home.

"When Lyle and I overheard our parents talking about losing the house," Lyle's older brother Ward said, "we both vowed, 'We'll buy it back for you!'"[13]

This unforgettable experience seared family loyalty and adult responsibility into Lyle's consciousness at a very tender age. He must have sensed his father's humiliation.[14] Yet he also learned from his father's quietly determined response to adversity—he watched his father maintain dignity and pride in the face of financial failure, a sense of integrity and obligations to creditors, and commitment to his family.

Afterwards, Anson moved his family to Kitchener, continued as a contractor, and founded Hallman Construction and Home Builders Limited.

When Lyle was in high school, he spent three years (1936 to 1939) at the Kitchener-Waterloo Collegiate and Vocational School—commonly called Kitchener Collegiate Institute or KCI—taking courses in the tech-woodworking department. (This foreshadowed his later involvement in home building and the construction industry.) His specialty was pattern-making. There are still iron joints in the front railings of KCI that were designed by teenaged Lyle out of wooden patterns.

In 1942, when he was twenty years old, contrary to his family's Mennonite pacifist tradition and to the chagrin of his parents, Lyle joined the Royal Canadian Air Force (RCAF). His brother Ward had enlisted a year earlier. Lyle received training as a wireless navigator and was commissioned as a sergeant in 1944. He was discharged at the end of World War II, in October 1945.

"This was the happiest day in my life! What a waste of time!"[15] he rejoiced.

Years later, Lyle understood that joining the RCAF—an organization that taught structure and discipline—during a very formative time of his life gave him skills that served him well during his building career. It also helped him mature, and he decided to go into business independently.

That same October, in 1945, Lyle established Hallman Construction Limited with $500 of his own savings and another $500 from his father. Although Anson still operated his own company, he increasingly worked on Lyle's projects.

An early family business pattern also emerged, an unspoken acknowledgement of differences in temperament between the two brothers, Ward and Lyle, and a growing difference of opinion on preferred types of construction. It led them in separate directions.

"I was always interested in commercial and institutional construction," Ward said. "Lyle was clearly committed to residential construction—houses and apartments."[16]

In 1947, after working for Lyle for several years, Ward moved to Nova Scotia, went into the building industry, and ended up working in design, construction, and maintenance for Sobeys, a national food retailer. He stayed there until he retired in 1982.

Back then, at the beginning of his business career, Lyle already displayed a penchant for careful analytics. He realized that the return on investment for residential construction was better than commercial construction, returning fifteen percent rather than five percent. Although he wasn't obsessed with profit and money, his father's experience in the 1930s and the effect on the family circumstances was not forgotten. Lyle knew that financial stress was ever-present in his father's mind, and he vowed that financial security would not be a constant struggle in his career.

His father used to say, "You can make a good dollar being a good carpenter, but you'll have to do more than that to buy ice cream."[17] Lyle embarked on his own journey of figuring out how to afford more ice cream.

Scarcity of money had led Lyle to an early interest in banking as a career. Then, he realized bankers were primarily conduits for money exchange.

"I saw a serious flaw in my earlier thinking," he said. "If the banker is so smart, why isn't he rich?"[18]

He soon progressed to a deeper examination of the entire building industry and arrived at a conclusion that became the secret to his success, and the foundation of the Hallman legacy. He embarked on a lifelong journey of building equity by buying land, a lot of land, which one could do rather cheaply at the time.

> "I began to realize that banking was not the place to be; the real secret was land. This became basic. Not 'he who has the gold,' but 'he who has the land!'"
> *Lyle Hallman*

Early on, Lyle clarified the strategic direction of Hallman Construction. First and foremost, he understood he was better at analyzing and organizing than selling and marketing. He believed in the passive but powerful role of financial capital, his ability to achieve concrete results, the importance of managing efficiencies, and the need to understand the marketplace.

One of Lyle's early insights concerned his own personality: "I'm not much for personal contact."

Lyle was obviously quite introverted. He could communicate effectively, but he did not have a lot of social interactions, and they were not something he necessarily enjoyed. Managing people, schmoozing customers, and joining countless committees were not things he naturally gravitated toward. He derived more energy from thinking and analyzing.

He simply enjoyed building—finishing a roof, seeing a house completed, and appreciating a job well done. He was internally motivated to achieve very concrete results. Building houses and apartments gave him a sense of accomplishment.

Lyle understood the advantage of having money and equity work for him, whether he was present or not. And so, almost from the beginning, he organized Hallman Construction so that he was not required to be constantly on-site. He was one of the first builders to extensively use subtrades while providing leadership as a general contractor. This allowed him to have very few people on his actual payroll and freed him up to use his analytic and strategic thinking to manage and lead.

Lyle enjoyed control; he relished making decisions. He grasped the importance of careful, well-organized, and precise management practices to drive profit margins. He understood and had the temperament needed to take calculated risks when necessary to accomplish long-term goals. He also had an intuitive understanding of the marketplace. His powers of observation and ability to connect different social phenomena led him to realize that housing needs would grow exponentially in the post–World War II era. He also committed himself to building homes for all.

"Whether building houses or rental units, we provide shelter for ordinary people at a reasonable cost."

This is what worked for him, and he stuck with this formula. As history shows, it proved rather successful.

DEVELOPMENT OF HALLMAN CONSTRUCTION

In 1990, when Lyle was asked to describe what he was most proud of in his business, he replied, "My first land purchase for development."[19] That purchase, which occurred in 1946, was the A. Shantz dairy farm, named Rosemount and located near Edna and Frederick Streets in Kitchener. Abraham Shantz was related to Lyle. Abraham's first wife was Emma Hallman, Lyle's second cousin twice removed through a common ancestor—Benjamin Hallman, Jr., the first Hallman settler to Canada. Benjamin was Lyle's great-great-great-grandfather and Emma's great-grandfather.[20] Those eighteen acres, still known as the Rosemount neighbourhood, were the site of the first subdivision Lyle developed.

Lyle was a pioneer and innovator, particularly in construction activity and property development. He progressed from building houses, to the construction of apartment buildings, to the development of land, and then to property management.

By the end of its first decade of operation, Hallman Construction was building more than 75 houses a year from Waterloo Region to Guelph to Oakville to what is now Mississauga.

It was the scale of Lyle's business activities, fuelled by his entrepreneurial mindset and careful planning, that set him apart from other builders of that era. He would buy tracts of land, subdivide them, and sell some of the building lots, which would help finance construction on the remaining lots by his own company. The scale of his building operations also meant that he purchased lumber and equipment in bulk and was able to employ subtrades efficiently and more profitably. He constructed his first apartment buildings in 1954, one with fifteen units and another with twelve units, on Brick Street. This was at a time when he was a new dad to a boy and a girl, with one more on the way.

Lyle built his first apartment buildings on Brick Street in 1954, one with fifteen units and another with twelve units.

Lyle and Dorothy Groff married in 1947, and their first-born, Peter, arrived in 1950. Soon following were their daughter, Susan, in 1952; their second son, Jim, in 1955; and Tom, their youngest, in 1961. But family life did not decelerate Lyle's business involvement. He helped form the Kitchener-Waterloo (K-W) Homebuilders Association (1948), managed the K-W Industrial Exhibition for three years (1952 to 1955), and was president of the K-W Junior Chamber of Commerce (1952) and secretary treasurer for Buildevco, a large land holding company (1954).

The concept of cooperation, particularly in the building industry, was not widely practised when Hallman Construction began. However, like so many Mennonite farmers in the surrounding vicinity who practised various forms of mutual aid, and in the spirit of barn raising, Lyle and thirty-three other local home builders organized themselves as Buildevco Limited to collectively compete for land to develop. This holding company was considered the largest land development company in Canada at the time.[21]

Lyle was one of the first five major investors. Each contributed $15,000 to Buildevco—at a time when $500 was the average price of a single lot. Lyle was also the founding secretary and, with George Tamowski as president, assumed major control of the holding company. Financially, Buildevco was a good investment for Lyle, and he enjoyed a profit of $150,000 after fifteen years of operation.

The Stanley Park subdivision in Kitchener, established in the 1960s, was the most significant development for Buildevco. It was built on more than 500 acres of farmland lying between Ottawa Street and the Grand River that had belonged to the Snyder family for well over a hundred years. St. Anthony Daniel Catholic Church in Stanley Park sits on the former site of the Snyder family home, which was a fine example of a typical Waterloo County farmhouse, with a gabled roof and a large, full-width veranda on the front. The St. Daniel Catholic Elementary School was also built on the farmland.

Lyle used the 1960s to accumulate land outside Kitchener as well. Because of his involvement in Buildevco, he and Tamowski agreed not to purchase land for their own companies in the Kitchener area. In 1961, Hallman Construction purchased a 150-acre farm on Highway 7 near Guelph; the original farmhouse remains the principal residence of a Hallman family member. Lyle eventually expanded his land purchases into all areas of Waterloo Region, including Galt, Cambridge, Preston, Guelph, Wellington County, as well as Kitchener.

It wasn't until 1967, when the company had begun its third decade of operation, that Lyle built the first of 75 buildings that became known as Hallman Apartments at 343 Mill Street in Kitchener. He soon realized that he had stumbled upon a winning formula for building multi-family dwellings that paved the way for even greater future growth. After buying a tract of land to be developed, he would set aside a parcel for future apartment construction. The future land cost of that parcel would be absorbed and covered by the profits from building homes and selling lots on the rest of the tract. Most of the multi-family buildings constructed by Hallman Construction were built on debt-free blocks of land.

On the occasion of the company's thirtieth-anniversary celebration in 1975, it was noted that "Hallman Construction Limited, a solid and successful building development company, builds and sells more than one hundred quality-built homes each year and now has built over one thousand apartment suites …."[22] Lyle was clearly recognized as a major property developer.

NEXT GENERATION COMES OF AGE

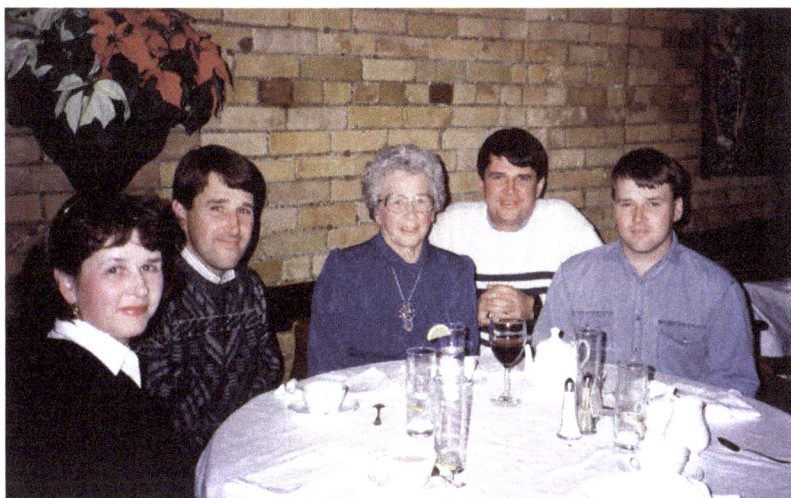

Dorothy Hallman with her children.
From left to right, Susan, Jim, Dorothy, Peter, Tom, [early 1990's]

By the time Lyle had "arrived" as a major property developer, Peter was already in his teens. As someone who came of age during the 1960s and '70s, Peter was shaped by the unbridled optimism that characterized the baby boomer generation. The world was an inviting place. Everything was possible. The future beckoned as a cornucopia of entrepreneurial possibilities. Being the oldest child, with a dominant personality and quick intelligence, he was propelled into the spotlight rather early.

Unlike his parents, Peter had little or no worry about survival or making ends meet. He grew up in a business family that clearly valued self-reliance and entrepreneurship. He was also nurtured in a Mennonite subculture that emphasized meaningful engagement with life and work and community organizations. This helped instill a lifelong commitment to service.

As a teenager and young adult, Peter was a constant presence on church softball and hockey teams. Because of his heft, which he didn't mind using, he fit in rather well with the Breslau Brawlers, as the Breslau Mennonite Church hockey team came to be known. His brothers, who played a more finesse game, affectionately described Peter's sports endeavours as involving more brawn than skill.

Many young Mennonites of his generation volunteered in the Mennonite Central Committee's Year of Service program, which involved living abroad for a year on a minimal stipend while engaging in meaningful community work. Peter was assigned to a group home for troubled children in Spring Valley, outside New York City. This early experience fuelled a passion for ongoing engagement with youth throughout his life.

Peter attended high school at Rockway Mennonite Collegiate, where he met Brenda Snyder. After a rather tumultuous courtship, they were married at Wilfrid Laurier University's Keffer Memorial Chapel in 1973 when Peter was twenty-three. They subsequently had three sons—Mark, Greg, and Brent—and adopted two girls, Nadine and Yves.

Peter Hallman's family. From left to right, (seated) Nadine, Gregg; (standing) Yves, Mark, Peter, Brent, Brenda, 1990s.

Immediately after the adoption of his two daughters in 1986, Peter was admitted to the hospital with what was thought to be appendicitis. His doctor soon called to explain the situation was much more complicated. He ended up remaining in the hospital for two weeks, diagnosed with a very severe case of Crohn's disease, and had a significant portion of his bowel removed. A close friend recalled suffering from a severe bout of ulcerated colitis himself and almost dying.

"One day in the hospital, I woke up in a fog," he said, "and Peter is at the end of my bed. Peter then told me, 'I came because you are in the same position I was in ten years ago, waiting for you to wake up so you can make a decision. With me they just took out most of my intestines. At least you are alive.'"

Peter made the decision that his disease would not prevent him from doing what he wanted to do. But he did suffer from chronic pain throughout his life.

Peter and Brenda always remained deeply committed to their church community. The young people from the College and Careers group would often gather in their home, and Peter, though older, identified strongly with the young people and their sometimes painful struggles to emerge as adults. He would send "amazing notes" of affirmation to those he mentored and visit them when they were as far away as Kentucky doing voluntary service.

Peter's natural leadership and his generosity were particularly felt by the congregation of Breslau Mennonite Church. A pillar of the church, he served on the church building committee, the youth ministry team, and the finance committee, and as a worship leader and Sunday school teacher.

Myriad stories of Peter's whimsical acts of kindness abound. Christian Aagaard, writing in *The Record*, told the story of a young friend laid up with a leg injury. Peter dropped by clutching a two-litre bottle of Coke, a bag of chips, and a copy of *Sports Illustrated*.[23] On another occasion he visited Marv Jutzi, a childhood friend and former hockey teammate who was in Freeport Hospital suffering from cystic fibrosis. Once again, Peter brought magazines and smuggled in some junk food.

"If there was something to be done," Laurence Martin, his pastor, said, "Peter did it."

GROWING UP IN THE MIDDLE

In many ways, Jim Hallman was a classic middle child. Growing up, he often found himself playing peacekeeper within the family, a common middle-child role. Between this role and developing in the shadow of a dominant older brother, Jim sometimes felt overlooked. Wanting to please and avoid rocking the boat, he became unassuming and patient. He was often underestimated, particularly in his studies, where his easy-going style was frequently misread as frivolity and a lack of seriousness.

But Jim demonstrated fierce ability in areas that mattered to him, particularly in sports, anything to do with motors, and later in his business endeavours. Like many other middle children, Jim was open to trying new things. He welcomed innovative alternatives and had the patience to listen and learn from experts. As a mediator within the family, he didn't agitate for leadership roles inside or outside the family. He also avoided depending on his family; he worked outside his father's business in his twenties and felt motivated to achieve his own unique accomplishments.

Jim enjoyed playing softball as a boy. Peter regularly dragged him along to games in their church softball league. Peter had created quite an aura around softball in the K-W region. He was always the front guy. Jim was "Peter's little brother."

Unlike his older brother, Peter, and his younger brother, Tom, who both went through some rough patches with their father, Jim always had a decent relationship with his dad. This gave him a lot of opportunities, particularly when it came to acquiring business experience. Although Lyle had always encouraged his children to "go do something else," Jim considered it "cool" to go into business. He started working at his father's firm during the summer as a high school student.

Yet, Jim never really felt trusted by either Lyle or Peter, and his father and brother did not help him along the way. He was never given much authority, although he always wished to be more involved. His business development therefore took a more roundabout path. He went everywhere in the company, acting as a jack of all trades. He wasn't the finish carpenter or trades guy. He wasn't the strong people person. He wasn't the numbers guy. But he always hoped his broad experience and general knowledge would come in handy someday. Ironically, he grew to become the family member with the most knowledge of the inner workings of Hallman Construction.

Jim finished one year at Fanshawe Community College in business, receiving his best grades in business law and computers. However, he was never that interested in formal schooling, probably because he was more practically focused. Some of that tendency may have been in reaction to his father, who thought education was everything. His biggest conflicts with his father growing up were over school and the grades he brought home.

"I realized that there were going to be a lot of A students working for C students," he said, in what would become a familiar quote.

He clearly fit a common pattern of many successful businesspersons who lack the desire for formal education yet develop the habits of a lifelong learner.

He went off to work at a number of other construction companies in Southern Ontario after graduation, returning to Hallman Construction in 1978 after the birth of his second child. By then, Jim and Sue Martin had married (in 1974) and had two children—the oldest was named Nathan; the youngest, Kerri.

At the time, Hallman Construction was building some houses but mostly apartments. Mel Bauman was Lyle's construction superintendent. Jim became Mel's right-hand man and was largely occupied with doing all the grunt work. By 1981, Jim had gradually moved on to managing properties, although his focus was primarily maintaining the company's apartment buildings. He still reported to Mel on construction projects but more generally answered to his father on maintenance of the Hallman apartments.

Jim on site at 37 Vanier, the last apartment built
by Hallman Construction in 1994–95.

The year 1978 also saw the divorce of Lyle and Dorothy after thirty-one years of marriage. In 1982, he married Wendy Guittard, who had started at Hallman Construction as his secretary/receptionist. While his second marriage to Wendy was a good one, Lyle deeply regretted the failure of his first marriage.

The next year, 1979, saw the completion of a ten-year subdivision project. In 1969, Lyle and lawyer Steve Cameron had begun working together on development of the Alpine subdivision in the south end of Kitchener, centred on Alpine Plaza. At the time, the land for this development was owned by Peter Bechtel. Lyle and Harold Freure bought the land and proceeded to divide up the parcel of lots over a five-year period. The entire development turned out to be a ten-year project. This initial collaboration cemented the start of a lifelong personal friendship and professional trust between Lyle and Steve. Steve Cameron would become central to many of the conversations regarding Lyle's affairs.

Another lawyer in what was then the Sims-Clement-Eastman law firm, Paul Grespan, began working more intentionally with Lyle's corporate business and land development initiatives. In 1987, Paul set up his own law firm, McCarter Grespan, specializing in land development, and Lyle moved all his land development work over to the new firm. Paul continues to provide legal services to Hallman Construction.

The role Steve and Paul played as Lyle's advisors in setting up both Hallman Construction and the Lyle S. Hallman Foundation would later create tension and confusion in the early years of the foundation.

CAPTAIN OF THE SHIP

Lyle relaxing on one of the many boats he captained over the years.

During the 1980s, Lyle was busy acquiring properties and land. Although this was mainly in Waterloo Region, it also encompassed property in Fergus, Listowel, and New Hamburg. Acquisitions were something he did primarily by himself. He loved looking for land, he loved negotiating for good land deals, and he loved stockpiling property. Lyle saw himself as the founder responsible for doing everything.

Both Peter and Jim would go driving with their father to check out potential properties—these were among their fondest memories. But when it came to thinking about and planning for the future, Lyle had difficulty trusting the next generation. How could they possibly know what it really took to amass an empire? He thought it would be much better for his children to receive money than to run the business he had created. He believed that if they came and worked for him, they would not have the opportunity to be as successful in their own right, and people would think their success was actually due to his success. He was going to be captain of his ship to the end.

By 1985, when the company marked its fortieth anniversary, Lyle had purchased 415 acres on Ottawa Street North in Kitchener, which lay between the existing Stanley Park community and the Grand River. Another tract, with 1,886 building lots and designated Hallman-Idlewood, was purchased along Old Chicopee Drive. A year later, in 1986, the company purchased another 250 acres in Pioneer Park for development. After forty years in the building industry, Lyle was developing several hundred lots and building 200 to 300 apartment units each year. Altogether, Hallman Construction developed over 750 building lots between 1986 and 1989. And between 1975 and 1985, the number of apartment units owned and managed by the company had grown from 1,000 to over 3,000.

Meanwhile, Peter was distinguishing himself in many voluntary leadership roles within Waterloo Region. He was not yet thirty when he became chair of the board of directors for the Canadian Mental Health Association in South West Ontario in 1999. Margaret Motz, who was the executive director of the association in the late 1970s, found it unusual for such a young person to both function as president of the organization and simultaneously demonstrate such thorough knowledge of the organization's goals. She thought Peter was a thoughtful, results-oriented leader who brought a caring human dimension to the board dynamics. During this time, Peter was also studying to become a chartered accountant, but his path toward serving the broader community in voluntary leadership was already firmly established.

From early on, Peter actively sought and engaged in civic and business leadership roles. These early forays into community leadership demonstrated a unique set of complementary strengths. Although he could be quite forceful, even brash, in his approach, he always listened to others very carefully. He was well trained as an accountant and found it easy to default into micromanaging staff and committees. However, he had formidable skills as a big-picture thinker and strategist.

As a result of Peter's many volunteer assignments, it was natural that he became involved with the regional Federated Appeal. John Thompson, the organization's director at the time, recalled that Peter joined the board at the age of thirty-four and became president of Federated Appeal in October 1984. Peter soon began questioning whether Waterloo Region and its Federated Appeal would not be better served under the Canadian United Way umbrella, which would help consolidate donations for worthy social service agencies.

Eventually, under Peter's board leadership and John Thompson's executive guidance, Kitchener-Waterloo became the 106th member community of United Way of Canada. With Peter's support, this national fundraising body had convinced the board that United Way could give the organization access to a more sophisticated infrastructure of skills programs, campaign strategies, and general oversight techniques. In 1977, twenty-seven agencies were funded by Federated Appeal. By the time John Thompson's tenure ended in 2005, more than fifty-six agencies were being funded at over $7 million annually by United Way. Thanks in no small part to Peter's leadership, United Way has become a very successful fundraising vehicle for social service agencies in Kitchener-Waterloo ever since.

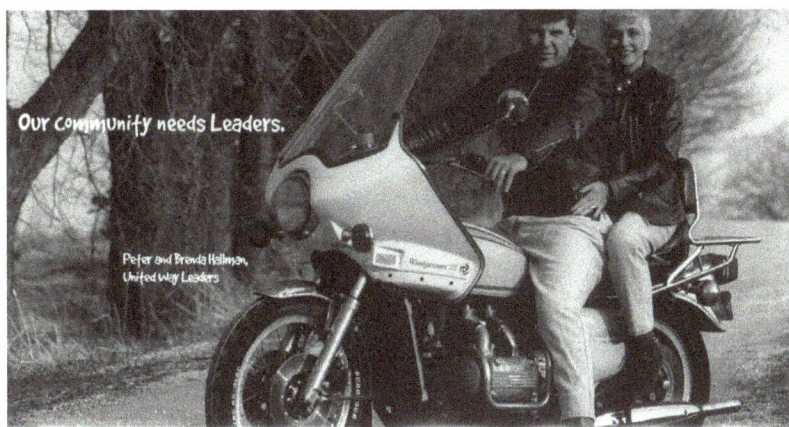

Our community needs Leaders.

Peter and Brenda Hallman,
United Way Leaders

Peter and Brenda Hallman, United Way leaders, 1990s.

In the late 1980s, Jim left Hallman Construction and started his own building company—K-Nat Construction. It was a miserable failure. Jim built a few houses and did some renovations, but he soon realized he didn't know enough. When the economy took a real downturn in the early 1990s, Jim approached his father about returning to the family business. Mel Bauman left around this time, and Jim took responsibility for the construction of apartment buildings. During this transition, Jim had a conversation with his father about the money he owed him. Lyle forgave the debt, considering Jim's entrepreneurial venture as part of his tuition costs.

"Lyle was always okay," Jim said, "as long as I was learning."

It had become painfully obvious to Jim that he needed help in order to make it on his own. He had never participated with Lyle in any facet of "deal making," and he had never had to worry about the financial end of the construction business. He had never had his own bookkeeping set up properly. Although he had always been a responsible employee, Jim became aware that he had never been taught, and didn't understand, time management. As a result, he began to pay attention to all aspects of running a business—with much more humility.

In 1989, Lyle reorganized Hallman Construction to try to "keep it all in the family." He appointed Peter as president and Jim as secretary-treasurer. Susan and Tom became directors, and Wendy became president of the property management division. Lyle himself was chairman. However, it seemed merely a paper shuffle to the family. The titles and responsibilities were never really put into action, and by the mid-1990s, they became meaningless. They would become obsolete by the year 2000.

UNIQUE LEADERSHIP STYLES

After Lyle turned seventy, in 1992, he expressed some thoughts about turning things over, just as his father, Anson, had done. But unlike his father, Lyle had more than just keys to put on the table. Lyle began to take an average of two weeks off each month. He was a young seventy and on his second marriage to a younger woman. However, although he talked about sharing responsibilities and having monthly meetings, it was clear to everyone that he still remained the boss.

During the 1990s, Peter simultaneously functioned as the senior executive of two family businesses: Hallman Construction and Hallman Eldercare. The path that took him there began with an undergraduate degree in economics, followed by an accounting degree at what was then Ryerson Polytechnical University, and a chartered accountant designation. He began his accounting career with KPMG in Kitchener, only to be named president of the reorganized Hallman Group of Companies by his father in 1989. In this leadership role, Peter became the key contact for all major financial and business deals, although his father maintained ultimate decision-making authority.

Peter Hallman at the official opening of Bankside Terrace, the first retirement home built by Hallman Eldercare, 1996.

At the time, Peter emerged as the more or less dominant Hallman in Waterloo Region. Much of the community recognition was well deserved and came out of a deep respect for his tireless volunteer work. But as with many successful leaders, his results-oriented style was at times resented as too pushy and domineering. The amount of press Peter received began overshadowing his father's prominence in the community.

Peter also served on the K-W Hospital board as a civic representative from Woolwich. It did not take long for him to be elected chair of the board. It was during a time of tumultuous change in provincial health care services. Talks had started between the K-W Hospital and the Freeport Hospital about achieving greater cooperation, but the facilities had two distinct mandates and cultures. K-W Hospital dealt primarily with acute care (severe and short term); Freeport dealt with chronic care (long-lasting and persistent). It was questionable if a merger that could retain the strengths and distinctiveness of both organizations was even possible. How could they achieve the provincially mandated economic savings of a potential merger without creating havoc among management? How could they prevent long-term resentment if the merger went off the rails? It was a politically loaded situation—and the kind of leadership challenge that suited Peter's skills.

In recognition of his emerging stature within the community, on November 18, 1994, he was appointed chair of a new transition committee that had board and senior staff representation from both hospitals. The possibility of monumental change was producing anxiety and volatility. Peter's diplomacy and tact allowed for both the venting of feelings and the creative development of new strategies and solutions. In his role as chair of the steering committee, Peter was a tireless consensus builder, making sure the work of the transition committee remained transparent. According to Al Collins, CEO of the K-W Hospital at the time, Peter "conceptualized the idea, worked with people to rally around it, and then encouraged the committee to do the work to bring it to fruition."[24]

Under his leadership, which was not without controversy, the committee achieved the merger of the two hospitals into a single organization—Grand River Hospital—with two sites, K-W and Freeport. Grand River Hospital currently serves Waterloo Region through a 665-bed hospital and fifteen specialized programs and services.

In December 1995, Peter was presented with a plaque recognizing his monumental service as chair by the Grand River Hospital Board of Trustees. Even individuals opposed to the final merger commented on

Peter's charismatic leadership as chair of the transition committee and how he maintained a light-hearted approach to serious topics. He was always up for a joke and could evoke much laughter. They also liked his detailed organization and quick response. If he didn't respond immediately, he could be counted on to call back within five minutes.

As for the middle son, by the early 1990s, Jim realized that if he remained at Hallman Construction he ran the risk of becoming seriously trapped. Gone was the optimistic assumption that his father would retire at some point in the near future. Jim concluded he could either stick it out and be miserable, or leave and do his own thing.

"Until I separated myself, I couldn't get along with Dad," he said—although, admittedly, this separation was a gradual and evolving process.

In 1995, Jim's independence reached another level, and he achieved this successful separation. He decided he was not going to rely on Hallman Construction to determine his future—he started his own construction company, Aberdeen Homes Inc., and launched a sideline, racing cars. In psychological language, Jim had taken another step of "individuating." Or, as he put it simply: "I matured."

The relationship between Jim and his father began to improve. Aberdeen as a business was working well, and Jim experienced the thrill of launching his own venture. His father no longer had any control. There were no financial ties. Nonetheless, Jim remained connected to the family firm legally, as Lyle insisted he retain signing authority at Hallman Construction.

Jim's older brother, Peter, had always nurtured the desire, demonstrated the aptitude, and displayed the drive to become Lyle's successor in leading the Hallman Group of Companies. Jim, as the middle son, seemed outwardly not as driven. He realized Lyle wasn't going anywhere. It was Lyle's business, and his father had complete and arbitrary power to do whatever he desired.

Jim was therefore not surprised by his father's "controlling from the grave" speech in 1998.

A TURBULENT DECADE

By the 1990s, Lyle had built up the biggest construction and property development company in the region. Looming on the horizon was the question of succession— how to transfer ownership and control to the next generation. However, once his sons were involved, it seemed he didn't really want to address this challenge in a straightforward manner. It became obvious to his children that he was having difficulty handing over responsibility, let alone engaging in a more transparent collaborative process of transition.

Having Lyle's second spouse in the business also became an issue that was harder and harder to ignore. Dynamics within a family business are complicated at the best of times. Before her marriage to Lyle, Wendy had been his secretary. As Lyle's spouse, her status and power within the office rose to compete with Peter's—it didn't help that Peter and Wendy were the same age.

Another complicating factor was that Peter, trained as a chartered accountant, managed all the company's finances and much of his work was done on a computer. Having grown up in a different generation with very different technology, Lyle had difficulty understanding what Peter actually did and tended to underestimate his contribution.

Generational differences showed up in other ways too. For example, Lyle made sure never to drive a Cadillac, which for him symbolized an overly showy type of opulence. Yet, on the other hand, he maintained his "toys"—a travel agency, a gold mine, and a succession of yachts.

A family business consultant had warned them a few years earlier: "There are too many Hallmans working here." It was not much fun working in an increasingly conflict-ridden office.

The internal conflicts became so difficult in the 1990s that Peter temporarily moved his office outside of Hallman Construction headquarters. It was during this same time that Tom also found the office too small for the four operational leaders, and he made plans to move completely out of his father's sphere of influence. He and his father privately negotiated what amounted to an early inheritance. Lyle "hived off" a block of apartment buildings (eleven apartment buildings with 600 units) in Cambridge for Tom to own and manage through his own company, which he continues to own and manage to this day.

Jim had a different relationship with his father than the other sons. He was once asked, "What is the key to your success?"

After a long and thoughtful pause—something he is known for—he answered, "Being able to disagree with my father, not follow his orders, and still enjoy lunch with him every week."

Conflict, insubordination, and enjoyment—they aren't usually combined to describe a vital relationship, particularly between a father and son.

> "My key to success was being able to disagree with my father, not follow his orders, and still enjoy lunch with him every week."
> *Jim Hallman*

LOOMING SUCCESSION CRISIS

In the winter of 1997, Peter was invited to participate as a panellist in an evening workshop on family business succession. It was hosted by the Mennonite Credit Union of Ontario and Conrad Grebel University College at the University of Waterloo.

"These were some of the best hours spent in my life," a number of local business leaders said.

The raw emotional intensity of the business family panellists struck a responsive chord among many participants. In follow-up conversations involving Peter and Milo Shantz of Mercedes Corporation in St. Jacobs, an idea was born to launch the Centre for Family Business in Southwestern Ontario. It was clear Peter understood the looming succession crisis facing not only his own family but many other family firms in Waterloo Region. He did not need statistics to tell him that family firms were driving sixty to seventy percent of Waterloo Region's economic activity. He was living that experience and was finely attuned to the needs and challenges of the many other business family members he engaged with throughout the community. In keeping with his community service orientation and leadership wisdom, he was all in.

Peter, along with community business leaders such as Milo Shantz of St. Jacobs, Rick Martin of Wallenstein Feed and Supply, Mike Dittwiller of Waterloo Printing, and fifteen other founding family firms joined together with initial corporate sponsors TD Bank, Miller Thomson, Deloitte, and Arca Financial Group to launch the Centre for Family Business. The expressed purpose of this organization was to assist member business families in navigating the tricky shoals of family business dynamics—dynamics that tended to erupt most forcefully during predictable succession scenarios.

Within a year, the Centre for Family Business was operating with a membership of about forty family firms. Peter became the first board chair, and the centre continues to present a Peter Hallman Mentorship Award each year to a person who embodies Peter's gracious and unselfish support to business families. The centre is one of the largest and most successful business family centres in North America, if measured by active membership.

Lyle had begun grooming his first-born early within his home-building company. As Peter gained more experience and education—and particularly financial acumen—he began to emerge as an invaluable driver in the growth of Hallman Construction. This brought Peter to the reasonable assumption he would lead the family business into the next generation. After all, in his reorganization of 1989, Lyle had appointed Peter as president of Hallman Construction. But the reality of their personal and business relationship was always somewhat rocky.

A watershed moment for the Hallmans occurred late in 1998. Lyle Hallman was invited to speak at the inaugural event of the Centre for Family Business. The event was intended to pay tribute to three local family-business founders: Lyle Hallman of Hallman Construction, Lloyd Martin of Wallenstein Feed and Supply, and Lorna Bergey of Bergey's Cheese.

After being introduced by their children, the three founders spoke on three themes: What motivated them? Why had they been successful? How were they working with the next generation? As anticipated, the third theme proved the most difficult and prompted the greatest variety of responses.

The event received front-page coverage in the business section of the *Kitchener-Waterloo Record* on October 14, 1998. The article was titled "In Praise of the Founding Generation."

Sitting around the Hallman table at the Westmount Country Club were most of Lyle's adult children and their spouses. They were perhaps the most curious to hear his answers to the three questions. In his responses on the panel that morning, Lyle spoke of a drive to succeed that was clearly motivated by the Depression-era bankruptcy of his own contractor father. He suggested that his success was the result of four factors: good timing in buying land, fiscal responsibility in not over-leveraging, an unwavering commitment to honesty, and the power of positive thinking. But it was when he responded to the third question— "How are you working with the next generation?"—that the meeting got especially interesting.

At the age of seventy-six, Lyle described his current role as an active CEO of the Hallman Group.

"A few years ago," he said, "I told them I was gradually going to retire. They thought I was going to be gone the next day. What a surprise they got."[25] Then he spent considerable time explaining that, for him, working in his office was actually relaxing, just like a vacation. The subtext was clear: "Why would I ever want to retire?"

He also explained how the Hallman Group was organized. According to Lyle, his wife, Wendy, ran the property management division; Peter ran the land development and administrative sides of the business; and Peter, Jim, and Susan were in charge of the seniors homes and services, which insinuated that the Hallman retirement homes were controlled under his corporate banner. His children viewed this as inaccurate.

Then Lyle explained he had set up the LSH Investment Company to function as a venture capital fund for next-generation business initiatives. He considered this a fair way to distribute the money he had earned.

"Children see there is this big pile of gold hanging from the ceiling," he said. "It is going to come down to them at the Hallman companies. That won't happen. They have to prove to me they can handle it. When they can handle it, they can get all kinds of money from LSH Investments to start a new business or expand the businesses they have."[26]

Lyle encouraged other founders to help their children, but only after the founders took care of themselves first.

"Don't sell or give everything to your children if you don't have enough to survive on until you die."[27]

Observing the scowling faces of the next generation at the Hallman table, someone quipped, "I guess your dad is going to run it from the grave?"

Many family business owners face one of two challenges when retirement and transition approaches. If they are the founder, they often have no road map to guide them along the transition journey often referred to as "succession." Or they may have endured a problematic transfer from their own father and are prone to continuing an intergenerational pattern in a way that can seem strikingly self-unaware.

Lyle's retirement and succession planning was clearly going to be different than his father's. Apparently, on the day he turned seventy—September 21, 1957—Anson drove his company half-ton vehicle to the office, put the truck in the garage, came into Lyle's office, laid his keys on his son's desk, and said, "Today is my birthday. I'm through."[28]

In a commissioned memoir, *The Lyle S. Hallman Story*, which documents Lyle's business and personal journey up to his seventieth birthday on January 14, 1992, there's an intriguing and rather ambiguous epilogue titled "The Day After." It muses about succession and how Lyle would handle retirement. He was keenly aware that the succession question was looming, but the only direct quote he gave was, "My biggest struggle will be gradually to give up control."[29]

> "My biggest struggle will be gradually to give up control."
> *Lyle Hallman, The Lyle S. Hallman Story*

For many men of Lyle's generation, the concept of retirement seemed like a vast abyss of "nothing to do." They equated personal identity with work production. Even contemplating the idea of retiring was a frightening proposition. It represented change, and change is often understood as a loss of something, rather than the embrace of something new. Too often they think, "Why should I embark on succession planning, which is making me feel as though I am losing my identity?"

The Hallman business family had entered the 1990s with three next-generation members—Peter, Jim, and Tom—actively involved in day-to-day operations yet without a clear strategic plan for the future. With the addition of their individual goals, desires, and expectations, this amounted to a recipe for conflict that would involve difficult decisions and significant changes as family dynamics became increasingly complex.

The event at the Family Business Centre had shown the next-generation Hallmans the future, and it was looking very familiar … and interminable. They felt their father's remarks that morning were full of factual inaccuracies and judgemental insinuations, and betrayed his lack of trust in them. His comments also confirmed his continued unwillingness to collaborate in any transparent and meaningful transition planning.

Lyle Hallman with his four adult children in the 1990's.
From left to right, Tom, Lyle, Jim, Peter, Susan.

At the time, these next-generation Hallmans had already proven themselves as accomplished, thriving adults. Peter (age forty-eight) was a certified accountant, managed all Hallman Construction finances, and considered himself the heir apparent. He had also become a prominent civic leader, chairing the recent merger of two large regional hospital facilities to create Grand River Medical Centre. He and Brenda devoted much of their time to nurturing teams in local and international softball settings. Susan (age forty-two), having been a community nurse working at St. Mary's on women's surgery and gynaecology and at K-W Hospital on paediatrics for a few years, settled in as a homemaker with three young children. Tom (age thirty-seven) owned and managed a portfolio of apartment buildings. Jim (age forty-three) had started Aberdeen Homes and launched his own home-building venture. He had also embarked on a time-consuming hobby of sports car racing and could be found playing hockey any number of evenings a week in various leagues around town. During the mid-1990s, through Peter and Brenda's entrepreneurial initiative, Peter, Susan, and Jim had become co-owners of a new venture in the retirement home sector organized as Hallman Eldercare, and they were in the process of adding their third retirement home—Terraces by Hallman—in Cambridge. They were an accomplished bunch.

By the time of Lyle's speech, each of his children had come to separate conclusions about the trajectory of their father's business empire and where they fit in the Hallman orbit. Tom had pulled out, seeing no meaningful future for himself there. Peter continued to believe he was best qualified to manage the Hallman empire in the future and still hoped his father would recognize and act on that insight. Susan was quite close to her brothers and, not being business-oriented, wanted no significant involvement in the Hallman business future. Jim understood his older brother's ambitions, though he shared some similar desires, and chose to put his energy into his own business, which he could effectively control and manage.

All three sons had worked at Hallman Construction at one time or another in the 1990s, at times even overlapping each other. However, after their mother and father's divorce, the dynamics of working together in one office became unsustainable. None of the Hallmans were wilting wallflowers. With a dominant father, together with Lyle's second wife, Wendy, and three headstrong siblings all working out of the same office, something had to change.

The Hallman clan in 1998. From left to right, (front row) Nadine Hallman, Kevin Rempel, Brian Rempel, Katelin Rempel; (second row) Sue Hallman, Brenda Hallman, Wendy Hallman, Susan Rempel, Kathy Hallman, Stephanie Machado; (third row) Jim Hallman, Peter Hallman, Yves Hallman, Lyle Hallman, Marvin Rempel, Dan Machado, Tom Hallman; (back row) Nathan Hallman, Mark Hallman, Greg Hallman, Brent Hallman, Kerri Hallman.

TRAGEDY HITS

On Tuesday, June 22, 1999, Peter invited his brother Jim and a friend, Larry Shantz, to accompany him on a motorcycle ride. It was not unusual for this small group to go on spontaneous bike rides. However, that morning, both men had scheduling conflicts and couldn't join Peter. He left alone.

No one knows exactly what happened. Peter was riding his Honda 750 Sports Touring motorcycle when it ran off the road north of Lanark near Perth in Eastern Ontario. The Perth detachment of the Ontario

Provincial Police concluded that he was likely descending a steep hill on a curve when the bike left the road. His body was discovered by passing motorists in the ditch along County Road 511 shortly afterwards. Peter was forty-eight years old.

Peter Hallman on his Honda, 1999.

For many people, the day of Peter's death is indelibly seared in their memories. Close friend Bernie Burnett was big-water fishing in Parry Sound when he received the message. John Fast was waiting for Peter to join him at the Waterloo Inn for an 8:00 a.m. meeting to discuss a joint workshop they were planning for—Non-Family Managers in Family Firms—when Lawrence Bingeman walked through the doors to break the news. Brenda was in the garden when two police officers on motorcycles came up the driveway. One asked her whether this was Peter's home. The other crossed the road to get their son Brent before they told her the terrible news. Long-time friend and colleague John Thompson made many of the early phone calls to friends. No matter who said it, the message had the same gut-wrenching impact.

"Peter is dead."

Ironically, John Thompson recalled Peter agreeing, at his request, to address a United Way meeting that Friday on the topic of Facing the Future.

By the end of the day, that unforgettable Tuesday, all the children and their friends had gathered—the house was packed. Friends from far and wide brought food, and all the food was eaten. Peter left behind his wife, Brenda, and five children—Mark, twenty-two; Greg, twenty; Brent, eighteen; Nadine, seventeen; and Yves, sixteen.

Jim Erb of the Erb and Good Funeral Home recalled that Peter had advised him, while he was renovating his funeral home, to ensure that the facility would be able to accommodate really big visitations. Little did Peter know that the first really big one would be his own. Eight hundred people attended his funeral, and more than 2,500 people came through the funeral home during five visitations.

Grieving begins with remembering. Whether it takes the form of an Irish wake, a funeral home visitation, or a memorial ritual held at a favourite wilderness location, most families, religions, and cultures have a way of memorializing those who pass from this life into the next. Peter's memorial service was held at Breslau Mennonite Church on June 26, 1999.

During the memorial service, the congregants witnessed a big black cloud overhead, which proceeded to unleash a heavy deluge over the reception tent set up on the grounds. By the time the service ended, the black cloud had moved on. Jim and Sue were walking to the edge of the cornfield beside the church and felt transported above it; they interpreted it as a message: "It's going to be okay."

Untimely tragedies have a way of encasing past events within impenetrable legacies of grief. Some remain unshared. Some are not acknowledged. Very few understand the impact of unresolved grief on future decisions and events. For some, the myth of Peter Hallman became a larger presence than his actual life. As someone commented, "It is tough to compete with a ghost."

"It is tough to compete with a ghost."

REMEMBERING PETER

Just before he passed away, Peter had been nominated to chair the church council of the Breslau Mennonite Church. He remained a strong supporter of Rockway Mennonite Collegiate, where he had attended high school; he had also served on their board. Terry Schellenberg, the principal at the time, noted that Peter regularly attended athletic events and occasionally spoke at faculty meetings, sharing his perspective as a business person.

Baseball was a big part of Peter's life. He particularly loved fastball. In fact, he loved anything to do with organizing sports events and coaching sports teams. Kids affectionately called him Coach, and his three sons unanimously described him as "very competitive" when asked why their father loved sports so much.

Peter was formally involved with several local softball teams. He sponsored the Waterloo Twins men's senior team based in Waterloo and, in 1998, was the driving force behind the formation and operation of the midget boys Hallman Cubs, which hosted that year's Canadian Championship tournament.

Larry Lynch, coach and general manager of the Waterloo Hallman Twins at the time, recalled that Peter, a Gordie Howe fan and former high school football player, did more than just write a cheque for his teams.

"Rarely do you find a sponsor that has a real passion for the game," Larry said, "and we found that in Peter." That passion for sports was also evident in his huge collection of sports memorabilia, including his cherished Wayne Gretzky jersey.

At the time of his tragic and untimely death, Peter was co-founder and president of Hallman Eldercare, which built housing for seniors; president of the Hallman Group of Companies, the enterprise his father had built; chairman of the K-W Community Foundation; and a recently appointed board member of Economical Insurance.

Reflecting on Peter's legacy and contribution to the wider community, Joe Mancini, founder of The Working Centre, said, "Despite Peter's short life, he grew into the role of a community leader based on his integrity and commitment to strengthen community organizations."[30]

On April 1, 2000, Peter became the first posthumous honoree in the thirteen-year history of the Mayor's Dinner, an annual event to thank individuals for their outstanding community work.

On April 27, 2014, Peter was posthumously inducted into the Waterloo Region Hall of Fame at the Waterloo Region Museum. It was noted that he had served as both a volunteer manager and corporate sponsor for baseball teams in Kitchener and Waterloo—notably the Waterloo Twins, Canada's longest-established men's fastball team. On that day, the Peter Hallman Ball Yard in Kitchener was named in his honour.

Peter was driven not only to achieve success but to achieve it at high levels. Defining and achieving success in both family and business contexts, however, proved difficult. He must have realized his father would never fully hand over the reins of Hallman Construction to him. Undoubtedly, he struggled with this fact, as his own energy demanded all or nothing. This surely helped drive Peter's entrepreneurial foray into retirement homes. He also wanted to undertake something for Brenda and his retirement. Before launching their first retirement home, Bankside Terraces, in 1996, they established a connection with Greg Neid, an industry expert who helped them learn how to operate within the retirement home sector.

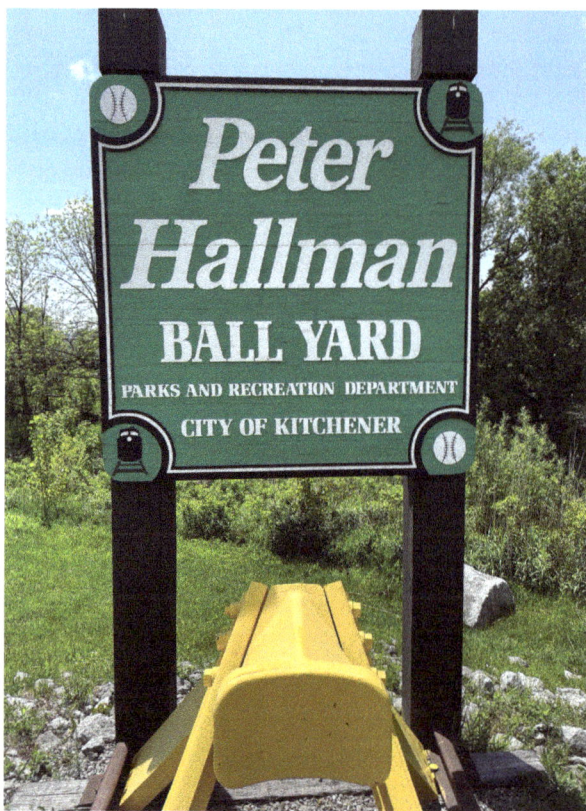

Peter Hallman Ball Yard in Kitchener

Groundbreaking ceremony for Bankside Terrace, 1996. From left to right, Brenda Hallman; Greg Neid; Grant MacDonald, minister at St. Andrew's Presbyterian; Peter Hallman; Bob Dyck, architect; Kitchener Mayor Richard Christy; Lyle Hallman; general contractor Rick Stevanus; Kitchener MPP and Ontario cabinet minister Elizabeth Witmer; Tony MacClean, elder care official.

Three months before his death, Peter, writing in the *Terrace Times*, expressed his anticipation and excitement as the company announced its expansion into Cambridge with the opening of its fourth retirement home, Queen's Square Terrace. He articulated two foundational principles: "our buildings will be operated as hotels rather than institutions" and "our customers will have maximum flexibility and choice." This would not be a regimented, rule-oriented institutional residence.

Peter and Brenda's new venture was an attempt to achieve two goals: to establish a "five-star hotel" atmosphere through relentless pursuit of excellence and to ensure the dignity and respect of seniors by allowing them to make more meaningful individual choices. Residents would maintain control over their lives. This last point was not generic marketing and branding triviality; it was a promise by Peter and Brenda of their active personal involvement.

"Our family lives on a one-hundred-forty-acre farm near Breslau," Peter proudly noted (Breslau being only sixteen kilometres from Cambridge). "We are family!" The retirement homes became Peter's signature attempt to merge the best values and characteristics of both family and business.

Peter Hallman was a meteor that burned brightly but much too quickly. His wife was fond of saying that Peter had lived three lifetimes by the age of forty-eight. Judging by the prodigious results of his activities, he may indeed have lived the equivalent of three lives.

"Settled" is not a description one would have attached to Peter during his life. He always seemed to be on the go, perpetually moving, right to the end. He achieved a great deal of success in a very short life as a dominant older brother, a prominent civic figure, a smart dealmaker, and a visible sports coach—he should have had more time to fully develop as a father, a husband, a business leader, and a family patriarch.

An African proverb summarizes well Peter Hallman's legacy: "A long life may not be good enough, but a good life is long enough!"

> "A long life may not be good enough,
> but a good life is long enough!"
> *African proverb*

Peter and Brenda Hallman, 1990s.

ESTATE PLANNING

Fathers expect to pass on before their children, not the other way around. When it does occur, it can short-circuit unrealized potential. Conflicts can remain unresolved. Hurts can linger. And the joy of growing old together is suddenly removed.

After Peter's death, Lyle's thinking around estate and succession planning changed drastically. According to his advisors, earlier in his life, Lyle had assumed his children would inherit and run his business. Now he asked himself, "How much money does anyone really need?"

Lyle had done an early inheritance deal with his youngest son, Tom, in the mid-1990s, when Tom received the apartment buildings in Cambridge. Peter's estate was settled upon his death. And although the value of some of Lyle's projects were frozen at the time—to establish their current value and fix the amount of any future estate taxes, which helps in estate planning—the bulk of his estate had not yet been assessed.

Lyle found the uncertainty around estate planning difficult. A simple concept began percolating in his mind. Peter and Tom had received their inheritances. Why not set up his other two children similarly and give the rest to the community? And then came the unforeseen sale of his apartments.

The announcement came out on June 10, 2003, and read as follows: "Hallman Sells Rental Empire."[31] At the time, Wendy was age fifty-three and the president of Hallman Property Management, and Lyle was eighty-one. Lyle and Wendy, who were among Waterloo Region's largest landlords, were getting out of the rental business, selling all of their more than 3,000 rental apartment units in sixty-three buildings. The move was described by many as the biggest real estate transaction ever in Waterloo Region. They made the deal with an out-of-town company, and it was concluded rather rapidly.

The signature Hallman buildings were solid, square, and basic, yet clean and always well maintained. They reflected an oft-quoted saying that had guided Lyle from the very beginning: "There are more Chevrolets on the road than there are Cadillacs." He had always prided himself on building "housing for the masses... geared to the average working person."

After the sale, John Whitney, a local real estate broker, summed up the impact Lyle had had on the region's real estate market.

"Hallman provided an infrastructure that allowed the region to grow … As other investors were turning apartments into condominiums, Hallman was adding to the area's rental housing stock. It would be hard to get the employee base we have and get accommodation for those workers without the units he built. What he built is as important as a road network or an expressway."[32]

Although he was pleased with the proceeds of the sale, Lyle commented that money has a way of disappearing. For the next six months, he spent considerable energy organizing his affairs and planning his estate. As he was trying to maximize the amount he could give to charity, the tax implications of the sale also began driving further estate planning.

MATHEW McCARTHY, RECORD STAFF

The Hallman family operates Terraces by Hallman and Aberdeen Homes of Cambridge and is one of the member families of the Centre for Family Business, based in Waterloo. At the Bankside Terrace retirement home in Kitchener are (from left) Sue Hallman, Jim Hallman, Kerri Hallman-MacDonald and Nathan Hallman.

(Jim and Sue Hallman, son Nathan and daughter Kerri
in front of a Terraces by Hallman Retirement Home)

As difficult as the succession challenge seemed to Lyle, history shows that the next generation is actually the most vulnerable. A front-page article in the *Kitchener-Waterloo Record* on October 22, 2003, titled "Resource for Family Firms: Non-Profit Centre Helps Parents and

Siblings Make Tough Decisions" served as a promotion for the Centre for Family Business. It was accompanied by a large photo of Jim and Sue along with their son, Nathan, and daughter, Kerri, in front of a Terraces by Hallman retirement home.

When Lyle read the article, he said, "Are you trying to upstage me by being on the front page of the *Record*?"

The article suggested that best practices for succession planning included a planning process inaugurated before the founder's sixtieth birthday—Lyle, of course, was now past eighty.

From a business ownership perspective, transitions are the last major management decision a leader ever makes—and succession usually determines the successful continuation of one's legacy. Lyle's succession plan was very simple and made without consultation. The underlying attitude was clear: "This is fair because I pronounce it fair."

Since Lyle felt he had already dealt with inheritance questions regarding his children, he began to fashion the outline of a philanthropic trust. Little did he know how timely this action would be.

Four days later, on the morning of Sunday, October 26, 2003, Lyle died on his way to church in New Dundee. He was eighty-one-years-old.

Lyle and Wendy always went to church on Sunday morning; they lived in Waterloo and attended services in New Dundee. On this particular Sunday, they were planning to leave for a trip and weren't ready. For that reason, Lyle set out to church on his own. In New Dundee, there lived a husband and wife, a bus driver, who regularly attended church together in Kitchener and who normally picked up people along the way. Yet on this Sunday, the wife decided to attend later than usual and on her own. Her husband returned and gave her the truck keys so she could go to town. The morning routines of both Lyle and the woman were disrupted in ways that left them driving alone in their vehicles.

Although we will never know exactly what occurred and why it happened, it appears Lyle crossed the centre line of the road and hit the woman's car head on. Both Lyle Hallman and Beatrice Holst died in the accident. Two of Lyle's children, Susan and Tom, attended Beatrice's funeral.

By the time of his passing, Lyle had cemented his legacy. Many business friends considered him a selfless philanthropist. Among his peers it was acknowledged that he wanted to leave a lasting legacy and show an example to other wealthy individuals to follow his example. Lyle did accomplish this by providing seed money for a trust, and then urging others to get involved.

Lyle Hallman receiving the Order of Canada
from Canada's Governor General, Adrienne Clarkson, 2001.

Lyle's legacy is also reflected in the numerous awards and honorary titles bestowed upon him during his life. Among these were the Order of Canada in 2001, an honorary doctor of laws degree from the University of Waterloo in 2001, and the Canada 125 Medal in 1992. He was also installed as a member of the Region of Waterloo Hall of Fame.

Lyle Hallman receiving honorary doctor of laws from University of Waterloo President David Johnston, 2001. Left to right: Val O'Donovan, Com-Dev founder; unidentified; Lyle Hallman; David Johnston.

In the end, Lyle was primarily recognized as a philanthropist.

Lyle Hallman's legacy is clearly much more than buildings. At the time of his passing, he was one of Waterloo Region's most generous philanthropists. During the 1990s, he donated $1.5 million to the K-W Health Centre, $500,000 to the Fairview Mennonite Home in Cambridge, $500,000 for a pool that bears the Hallman name in Kitchener's Stanley Park neighbourhood, and $1 million to the K-W Community Foundation. Shortly before his death, he was at a ground-breaking ceremony to launch an addition to the Lyle S. Hallman Institute for Health Promotion at the University of Waterloo.

In the end, Lyle was primarily recognized as a philanthropist.

PAGE 16 - KITCHENER MARKETPLACE - WEDNESDAY NOVEMBER 22 1989

The Kitchener and Waterloo Community Foundation last week received a $1 million gift from Lyle Hallman, President of Hallman Construction Ltd. Here, Walter Bean, Honorary Chairman of the Foundation (left) and Ken Murray, Past President of the Foundation (right) accept the cheque from Hallman (centre). The Kitchener and Waterloo Community Foundation aids charitable, educational and cultural groups in the Twin Cities.

Lyle donating $1 million to the Kitchener and Waterloo Community Foundation, November 22, 1989.

COMPLEX RELATIONSHIPS

Expressing love, affirmation, and mutual caring did not come naturally for the Hallmans. There was a lack of harmony. For the men in the male-dominated Hallman clan, communicating about emotions was hard to begin with, and the actual expression of love was often difficult. Showing their mutual caring and concern for each other was not something they attempted regularly, and this did them no favours during the turbulent 1990s. Working through conflict, communicating collaboratively, exercising the emotional strength to respect and affirm each other—this was not found in abundance. Children can suffer because of it. Yes, there was love, but it seemed somewhat handicapped in its application.

This made it more difficult to express grief after both Peter and Lyle died suddenly, tragically, and in quick succession. Their unexpected deaths left their families, the organizations they were involved with, and their close friends stunned and suddenly bereft of their friendship and leadership. It also focused a spotlight on a very complex relationship that many wished had received more time, more grace, and more wisdom in order to mature into fulsome health and productivity.

Peter and Lyle's relationship was terminated by Peter's tragic death. His wife, Brenda, witnessed first-hand how stressful it had been for Peter to be the first-born son of Lyle Hallman. Peter and his father seemed to be in constant competition with each other. Neither would ever give up. Peter's siblings would describe both men as extremely stubborn.

Catherine Motz, a member of the Motz family that founded and owned the *K-W Record* newspaper, recalled serving with Lyle on the board of K-W Counselling Services in the early 1990s. Lyle had been a founder of the organization and was a fifty-year lifelong member of its board. She remembers him as an important voice around the table, wanting to state his piece when appropriate, not needing to dominate but also not to be silenced when he had an opinion. When he did speak, Lyle usually got to the very heart of the matter. It was obvious how carefully he had been listening—directly and vigilantly.

Sitting beside him at board meetings, she recalled, "I became very aware of both his conscientiousness and his quick sense of humour, which came out in his word play and quick wit. His approach to philanthropy was always so practical, and the following exchange illustrated his business-oriented view of assisting people: 'Can't we give these people a toothbrush and get them to brush their teeth?'"[33]

Peter also could be occasionally blunt—to the point some people might have considered it heartless. But many experienced him as very sensitive and even somewhat thin-skinned. Particularly around fastball, Peter did have a mean reputation and a "tough guy" image. Yet, as a friend commented, "If you didn't know him you would say, 'This guy is tough,' but you could really see the good in him … He was a really big teddy bear."

Peter's sons were often embarrassed by their father's penchant for telling baseball umpires what was right and wrong. Peter knew the rules and always carried a handbook, but as a coach he was frequently ejected from softball games because he argued incessantly with the umpires. He came prepared for those occasions, always bringing a newspaper along so he could retreat to his car and enjoy reading the news. Peter clearly envisioned eventually going into business with his three sons. His family laughs at that idea now.

"It never would have worked out. Dad was way too controlling."

Peter was also well known for his wicked sense of humour. One time, his good friend Paul Grespan had scored platinum seats at the Air Canada Centre for a Toronto Raptors basketball game, and invited Peter and two of his boys to come along.

Early the next day, Peter called Paul. "Have you seen the *Globe* this morning?" he asked. On the front page of the newspaper was a photo of Raptors star Damon Stoudamire stuffing the basket, and clearly identifiable behind him were Paul, Peter, and the two boys grinning from the sidelines.

"Aren't you glad we didn't take our girlfriends to the game?" Peter joked.

He also had an uncommon dose of empathy. He could listen intensely and attentively, and people found they came away from almost any conversation with a helpful suggestion, some encouragement, and a sense that he was in their corner. Those who were involved in projects with Peter recall they always felt listened to. He reached out very deliberately to friend and foe alike.

"Peter truly built bridges, not fences," one of his friends said, "and Peter was usually uber-involved. One could never accuse him of being just a spectator. He engaged charismatically, and when engaged, he was completely committed. Failure was not really in his vocabulary, and any lack of success was usually reframed as a learning experience."

He felt a strong drive to give back to his community, whether by serving on boards or through donations. This had been modelled by Lyle, and Peter nurtured it more deeply within his faith community.

In 1992, Peter gave his father a card for Father's Day with the following note penned inside:

Dad:

I am sorry for both of us that we are unable to be together this Father's Day. I understand this is a difficult time for you and I, no one said it would be easy. If I am unable to live up to your expectations as a person or as a businessman, I understand your concern. I ask only that you respect me for who I am. Through all of this, you remain as my father and that cannot be changed. I love and respect you both for who you are and your accomplishments in your personal and business life. I also thank you for guidance and care during my youth when my values and personality were being formed.

Love, Peter

How Lyle responded to his son's card and note remains forever between them; however, upon Peter's passing, Lyle said the following:

"Farewell, with love, to my son who led a full life and had a tremendous impact on many local and worthwhile organizations. You inspired many people in forty-eight years of life to move to greater and higher goals. You will always be missed."[34]

Peter eventually received his father's blessing, albeit posthumously.

A FATHER'S BLESSING

Four generations of Hallmans, fathers and sons.
From left to right, Anson, Lyle, Jim, Nathan.

A man is not a man until his father tells him he is man.

At a most basic level, you feel "blessed" when you have the assurance that you are appreciated and respected. There is an old proverb that claims 'that a man is not a man until his father tells him he is a man.' Lyle's relationship with his son Jim encompassed a version of this truth. In his own way, Lyle let Jim know that he believed and trusted in his fundamental goodness and that he was proud of him and wished him well on his journey. Every child needs that blessing from important adults in their life. Significantly, it also became the fundamental basis for the stated vision of the Lyle S. Hallman Foundation.

"Every child is supported by a caring adult."

Jim with his mother, Dorothy, on the *Queen Elizabeth II* transatlantic cruise, September 10, 2001. They disembarked a day before 9/11.

"How would you measure your success?" is a question Jim has heard in multiple various versions.

If he is in a light-hearted mood, he would laughingly answer, "I am not addicted and I am still married."

As a long-standing member and board member of the Centre for Family Business, Jim well understood the deeper challenges facing business families. The classic pattern of the next generation struggling to achieve independence within the family company, and subsequently descending into various destructive habits, is well documented in family business research and literature:

> On the one hand, adulthood requires independence and self-responsibility. However, working within the family business context too often prolongs the dependence of the next generation. If this tension is not resolved constructively by the ages of around thirty-five to forty, the son often moves into mid-life crisis mode. The inability to resolve such identity challenges—that is the failure to find his genuine voice within the family business system […] invariably leads the son to feel he has a limited number of genuine choices. And too often his sense of being trapped within the family business leads him to choose escape patterns that end up as destructive patterns.[35]

Though Jim faced the challenges of being one of the "next generation" as he journeyed into adulthood, he found his own voice and his own way of dealing with people. The positive trajectory of his own relationship with his father helped him realize later in life that "most of my relationships have ended up positively." Fond recollections of his relationship with his father show this.

"It wasn't until right after Peter was gone that Dad and I really connected," Jim said. "He needed the help and I suppose to the extent that he could even go there, he did emotionally trust me. The last time we were together at his cottage, Dad asked me to go get the boat ready. We drifted around the Muskoka lakes—eating ice cream here, french fries there—it was one of our last times together and a great memory.

"Dad and I would always have a weekly lunch. One week he asked, 'Where do you want to go?' We hadn't been at the Harmony Lunch diner for about thirty-five years, so we went downtown Waterloo and just really enjoyed a father–son time—just two guys sitting having a drink. We talked nothing deep and earth-shattering, just two guys, just bullshit. He liked watching sports, so we swapped the latest comments on our favourite teams. I would tell him about stuff I was doing and I would ask him about stuff he was doing. Nobody was trying to control anybody.

"Another time I said, 'Dad, come down and I want to show you a property.' Often he would offer an affirmation, saying, 'That's a good one.'

"Our last Friday lunch together was at the Whale and Ale on Victoria Street. As we were eating lunch, an acquaintance from our motorcycling group happened to come in. He was a high school teacher from Baden, who was part of a regular group of around ten bikers who we had gotten to know over the years. I chatted to him for a while and introduced him to Dad. That Sunday, two days later, Dad died in his tragic car accident. This guy came through the receiving line and he was really broken-up and said, 'Jim, I saw you and your Dad together, enjoying each other's company so much—it really moved me.' It struck him how much Dad and I were together. It is one of those things that has stayed with me.

"To have come that far—it meant a lot because at one time I didn't care whether he lived or died. I realize there are no guarantees in life, and I have no regrets—if Dad would have died and I didn't try everything I could to make it good between us, I would have felt really bad."

He recalls how much he enjoyed going to stock car races with his father when he was younger. They went to several wrestling matches for similar reasons—simply to spend time together.

By the time his father passed away, Jim had internalized confidence from their relationship because it ended positively. He now had the creative energy to move on and tackle other projects.

"If I hadn't had the chance to do my own business, like Aberdeen, and be successful," he acknowledged, "I probably would have been too anxious to take on the foundation project, particularly as it was facing its initial structuring challenges. And if I wouldn't have experienced Dad's blessing, I would not have had the strength to fight for what I believed was the best for the foundation in its battle with the PGT [Public Guardian and Trustee]."

In an insightful September 2005 article in the Making a Difference section of *Exchange Magazine* titled "Stepping Up to the Plate: Jim Hallman Continues a Family Tradition of Entrepreneurship, Philanthropy and Fastball,"[36] Brian Hunsberger described Jim as a designated hitter for the Hallman family. The article highlighted the unexpected leadership challenge that landed in Jim's lap after the tragic deaths of his brother and father. What made Jim's contribution so unique, Hunsberger observed, was that he had established his own track record of business success before being thrust unexpectedly into leadership roles with Terraces by Hallman and Hallman Construction. The article also noted the general lack of knowledge regarding the nature and depth of Jim's major involvements at the time. Jim's role as president of Hallman Construction required massive and careful attention. It was also a role that required a clean-up hitter.

The Hallman's foray into retirement homes was given its initial entrepreneurial impetus from Peter. Jim was able, through his subtle yet tenacious leadership, to solidify the focus and profitability of the new business venture. His own personal philanthropical track record was marked by humility, evidenced through anonymous donations. Some of Jim's close friends knew of his generosity, but many others were not aware of the charitable contributions from both him and his wife—and that is entirely the way Jim wanted it to be.

Intentional humility marked his leadership style in both business and philanthropy. This stood in marked contrast to the more public personas of Peter and Lyle. However, Jim's style of leadership proved to be just as effective, even as it was different.

As the insightful article noted: "If put in a baseball lineup today, Jim would most likely be put in the 'clean-up hitter' role." More than fifteen years ago, Hunsberger identified what have continued to be the hallmarks of Jim's leadership style—humility, tenacity, and results-orientation.

In one of the classics of business literature, *Good to Great: Why Some Companies Make the Leap and Others Don't*, there's a chapter on the topic of leadership that is worth the price of the book. After a careful examination of what distinguishes great companies from the merely good, author Jim Collins concluded that the two hallmarks of the leaders of organizations that achieve greatness are humility and professional will.[37] Jim Hallman's record as a leader clearly embodies these qualities.

However, Jim also adds "fun" to that leadership equation; his two recreational passions—car racing and softball—prove this.

FUN, HARD WORK, AND SUCCESS

"Happy drivers go faster."
James Kearney

Jim loves racing cars. He tells the story of going for a walk with Sue at age forty and confessing: "I am going to have a mid-life crisis—it's either a girlfriend or car racing."

Today, Sue laughs, "It should have been a girlfriend. His mid-life crisis would have been over sooner."

And although he was never a "gear head," Jim remembers always liking "anything with a motor that was moving."

He had always wanted to try racing but felt he should wait until he could do it properly—which meant waiting until he had the time and money to support the habit. And so, at age forty, he began researching the different classes of racing and talking to "racing guys" about the commitment it took to get into car racing.

Today, Jim sheepishly admits, "I am now among the faster drivers in the series that I race, and sometimes I get a trophy—but I just drive for fun. I do keep my records and try to improve."

He pursued his new car-racing hobby just as he tackles most of his projects and assignments—very deliberately, strategically, and with humility. It took him ten years to become competitive.

"I was dead slow at the beginning and lots of crashes."

By 2012, he was achieving success because he had acquired insight, skills, and knowledge. This pragmatic learning approach worked. Jim attributed his peak performance to five factors: good personal and working relationships with his team of experts (coach, mechanic, and pit crew), realistic goals that were not overly intimidating, reasonable confidence in his ability to achieve those goals, clear and direct lines of communication, and of course, a sound and solid race car. Of these five attributes, four were about emotional intelligence—just one was related to the mechanics of an actual race car.

Jim knew how to choose a team. He allowed each member of the team to contribute their best, and he was humble enough to listen to the experts among his racing acquaintances.

"The nice bonus to making gains, no matter how incremental," his racing coach, James Kearney, said, "is that the whole team is happy. And happy drivers go faster."[38]

After a particularly successful sports car qualifying session at Road America, Jim walked by his coach, grinning from ear to ear, and said, "That was easy!"

Jim Hallman, a middle-aged businessman, had just qualified seventh fastest in a highly competitive semi-professional race, the 2012 Runoffs at Road America, travelling over 150 mph through fourteen turns of the track.

With careful coaching, he had been able to shave 0.1 second or 0.2 seconds off many of the turns. His coach had planned for Jim to attempt a 1.1 second total improvement—an expectation his coach considered "nothing to sneeze at." Now Jim was basking in a 3.1 second improvement, which moved him from 11th place for qualifying up to 7th place to start the race. By the end of the race, he finished in 4th position. Jim felt hugely successful, and it clearly wasn't just about winning the race.[39]

The Hallman name has been attached to fastball in Kitchener-Waterloo for more than forty years. Jim enjoyed playing softball as a boy, and of course Peter regularly dragged him along to games. Jim also helped coach youth softball teams. Both he and Sue participated in the sport, and early in their marriage they became involved in sponsoring the women's Kieswetter teams. Eventually they became involved with the International Softball Congress (known as the ISC).

When asked why, they will simply say, "We just loved watching the game. And we developed so many friendships through softball." Jim also found that when he wasn't involved in sponsorship, the games were not as meaningful. Winning was so much more fun when you were involved with putting the team together, from management to coaching, and got to know the individual players.

Jim coaching in Kitchener Minor Softball in the late 1980s

After Peter passed away in 1999, Jim and Sue led a family-based group that was committed to Peter's earlier vision of success. But Jim faced some immediate challenges. Peter was a rather dominant and charismatic person, and it was initially tough to compete with his brother's reputation. When Jim came along, following his brother, he often faced the comparative question, "What does Jim know?"

"The most difficult thing was getting the respect from the local people regarding softball. I was able to do this under different terms and times than when Peter was around. The emphasis had been more local and I took it more on to the international stage through ISC. And with time and much effort, together with positive outcomes, I was able to gain the acceptance of local fastball people."

When he first became involved in softball, he was often underestimated and disrespected, and he had to make some hard decisions, particularly regarding personnel. His approach was to surround himself with good people and let them make things happen. As a sponsor, he stayed out of day-to-day management and focused on the bigger picture, the high-level decision making.

Starting in 2002, Jim and Sue began co-sponsoring the Waterloo Twins, one of the oldest active senior softball teams in Canada. The team immediately finished the season in third place. By 2005, Jim had taken over primary sponsorship and, in addition, created the Kitchener Hallman Twins. They also finished third at the ISC World Tournament in Wisconsin. With Jim's support, Kitchener-Waterloo hosted the ISC World Tournament in 2002, 2006, 2007, 2014, and 2018. In 2008 and 2009, Jim's Twins became just the second Canadian team to win the highly competitive ISC championship—two years running. In 2010, the renamed Hallman Twins came close to a three-peat but lost in the final in Michigan. Over a fifteen-year span, the team achieved eight first-place, second-place, or third-place finishes in the ISC World Tournament.

For his record of achievement, Jim was inducted into the World Softball Hall of Fame in 2018—although it nearly killed him to attend the ceremony and receive the actual recognition. He received the Bob

Welby Memorial Recognition of Service Award, a special branch of the ISC Hall of Fame reserved for "individuals who have distinguished themselves through contributions of their time, talent and treasure to the International Softball Congress and fastpitch softball in general."[40]

Hallman Twins, first-time ISC World Champions,
Jim and Sue Hallman with Larry Lynch.

As sponsors, Jim and Sue's leadership style was characterized by a get-it-done enthusiasm. Whether they were contacting additional sponsors, delivering posters, loading up supplies for the concessions, chasing foul balls, or serving as a games controller, Jim and Sue always added a personal "Hallman touch."

"While the championships and wins are great," Jim said when receiving the award, "it is the people we have met and worked with who I will continue to remember. The great people/players who have worn the Twins jersey during my time. The great people behind the scenes. The many managers and coaches we have had. Getting to know the families of the players. The golf games, the fun and enjoyment of playing a game we love. The tears and the joy."

And he was quick to deflect praise and acknowledge other key individuals who have helped with softball in Waterloo Region, including Dave Bailey, Larry Lynch, Robert Nydick, Brad Thomson, Doc Simmons, Doug Eidt, Steve Kooser, and Ron Hackett.

Jim and Sue with the Kitchener-Hallman Twins together with the Kitchener Cubs. Both teams were sponsored by the Hallmans.

Success was not only about winning but about doing it the right way and always with the right team players.

Todd Martin was the Twins' go-to pitcher for many years. He said he knew he had turned a car guy into a softball guy when he saw Jim celebrating enthusiastically after an early third-place finish.

"I knew we had him."

Jim's tales of his softball involvement always start with "we": "We put together really good teams… with really good guys… We didn't ever accept assholes as players." For Jim, success was not only about winning but about doing it the right way and always with the right team players.

During a game in Michigan, Jim overheard a spectator pointing at him and saying, "There is the owner of the Twins." The comment really bothered him.

"It makes me feel the opposite of good and proud," he later said. "It's not about the recognition for me… This is not my driving force." The idea that the drive for high achievement does not require the need for recognition is a hallmark of Jim's style of leadership.

> "It's not about the recognition for me."

For Jim, success meant striving for excellence, not just settling for average. His natural drive has always been toward peak performance in all of his endeavours. In his words, "You don't want to spend your life bemoaning what you lack."

> Success meant striving for excellence,
> not just settling for average.

CLEAN-UP HITTER

I n baseball, the fourth batter in the batting order is usually a power hitter known as the "clean-up hitter." The job of the clean-up hitter is to bring home any preceding hitters who manage to get on base. Although they tend to lead their teams in RBIs (runs batted in) because of the many opportunities they have to drive in runs, they are also known for having some of the highest strikeout totals as well as a low on-base percentage themselves. Without stretching the baseball metaphor too far, Jim stepped up to the plate as the clean-up hitter, often and well.

After Peter died in 1999, Jim had to clean up a lot of "bases." Jim's continuation of the Hallman softball legacy in Kitchener was perhaps the most personally enjoyable RBI. Other RBIs included providing leadership for the Hallman Terraces retirement homes; taking over leadership of the Hallman Group of Companies; transferring management of his own construction company, Aberdeen Homes; winding up a series of Lyle's extended business ventures; and perhaps his biggest challenge, establishing the Lyle S. Hallman Foundation.

Any one of these leadership challenges could have been a full career. They landed on Jim's plate in rather quick succession. But he first stepped up to the plate in the late 1990s and continued to hit a series of home runs.

Jim will say, "I got lucky." In reality, he evolved over time to become an effective leader through a convergence of his personal capacities, life circumstances, and opportunities. Effective leadership is highly situational. In Jim's case, his career trajectory was "situational clean-up hitter."

Fortunately, Lyle had things in relative order before his death. When his will was read, Susan, Tom, Jim, and lawyer Steve Cameron fully understood that the estate inheritance questions had already been resolved. In the early 1990s, Lyle had set up a family trust. After Peter's death, that trust was dissolved, with Lyle taking half and the remaining children set to receive the other half upon his death. Lyle's will mainly concerned two legal entities: the existing Hallman Construction company and the new foundation.

During Jim's younger days at Hallman Construction in the early 1990s, he was regarded as "the fixer."

"Dad had me in his back pocket," Jim recalled, "in order to fix those deals that weren't going well."

Fixing things began early in a very practical sense for Jim. Before starting his own construction company, Aberdeen Homes, he drove to Toronto to repair a building for a travel agency Lyle had just purchased. Like many other successful entrepreneurs, Lyle believed that if he could be successful in one business venture then he could hit a home run somewhere else. People could talk Lyle into business deals once they knew how to do it. And so, Jim's role moved from literally fixing to more figuratively cleaning up.

As executor of Lyle's estate, Jim had to tidy up some not insignificant ventures. One of them was Barg Management Inc. For several years, Lyle had financially backed his nephew, Gerry Barg, in what became Barg Automotive. (Gerry's mother was Lyle's sister, Jean.) Gerry had begun selling cars curbside in 1989 during his high school and early college years. The one-person operation grew to a multi-level automotive enterprise specializing in late-model pre-owned vehicle sales, service, and financing that employed more than 200 people at eleven locations in six Southern Ontario cities. It was quite the ride. Under the umbrella of Barg Management Inc., Gerry developed, owned, and managed Barg Automotive, AutoSure (insurance), OAC Leasing (financing), Cambridge Mitsubishi, Cambridge Kia, City Chevrolet, and Carsumer (Canada's first car e-dealer). When the estate was settled, the remaining next-generation Hallmans, Jim, Susan, and Tom, wound down the sixteen-year, mutually beneficial partnership between their family and Gerry Barg.

Beyond the family business connections, the larger clan of Hallman men bonded around one thing—cars! At Barg Automotive, Peter's sons, Mark, Brent, and Greg, worked with their cousin Gerry for many years managing various divisions.

After Gerry transitioned from the business, Peter's three sons started up their own used car lot on Victoria Avenue called Grand River Motors. For quite some time they entertained the thought of setting up more car dealerships.

At one auspicious Thanksgiving gathering at their mom Dorothy's home, one of the young men announced, "We have a Corolla in our back lot at Victoria Avenue that we plan to wreck. Anyone want to come?" To the uninitiated, "wreck" is code for setting a house on fire so you can get practice putting out fires.

The announcement caused quite a stir, and Jim and his son Nathan quickly joined Peter's three sons as they marched to the back of the Victoria Avenue car lot.

The wrecking was no haphazard effort. They carefully drained all of the oil out of the Corolla. Then they proceeded with the "wrecking process"—completely unaware that black plumes of smoke were coming out of the back of the shop ... until they heard the blare of sirens charging down the street. A series of firetrucks pulled into the car lot along with multiple police cars, their lights flashing and sirens blaring.

Lucky for the Hallman males, one of the police officers on the scene happened to be a friend of the boys—and also their second cousin.

"What the hell are you guys doing?" he roared.

"Just having some fun, officer," came the cheeky reply.

The rest of this story is locked within the annals of Hallman apocryphal history.

There were other situations where Jim was required to clean up after his father's death. There was Belgage Building Supply, a building supply company in the rear yard of the Hallman Construction office on Gage Avenue that Lyle was once talked into purchasing. There was Regal Brick, a brick plant located on Shirley Avenue that produced paving stones—a product Lyle thought might benefit his construction company; although Aberdeen Homes did buy some product from the company, their prices were never really competitive. Jim terminated the venture by selling the manufacturing equipment to buyers in British Columbia.

Lyle had the resources to play around and get involved in what amounted to hobby businesses. And it didn't bother him as long as Hallman Construction wasn't missing any paycheques. He also bought a Filter Queen franchise because he had purchased the company's products for his apartments and was under the impression he could get deals, even though those deals never materialized. He bought a travel agency for the same reason. It became another business that Jim had to shut down.

In the mid-1990s, Lyle bought the rights to a gold mine in Northern British Columbia. It was one of his more exotic business ventures. He kept a gold ingot from the mine on his office desk and proudly showed it to all visitors. The gold mine was located near Atlin, a remote community populated by Oscar winners, a judge from San Francisco, and other notable figures who relished their anonymous, off-the-grid lifestyle in the wilderness settlement. However, the mine lost millions. Beginning in the spring of 2004, Jim travelled to Atlin twice a year to supervise the operation. Lyle owned all claim rights and had financed everything, but finding a reliable mine manager took time. Jim landed upon a man he described as the "unofficial mayor of Atlin." This individual was highly knowledgeable about the industry and helped achieve a transition that led to earnings in the form of royalties. Eventually Jim sold the gold mine to the operator next door. He was relieved to give up the long flights and the grind of managing the operation.

"I just didn't have gold running in my veins," he said.

Starting in 1999, Jim also found himself stretched to the limit by two of his own ventures—Hallman Eldercare and Aberdeen Homes. Both required serious attention.

The Hallman Eldercare's Terraces in the Square residence had opened in 1998. It was a showcase retirement home in uptown Waterloo. It gave notice to the long-term care sector that the Hallmans were serious about becoming significant players in this arena. The genesis of moving into long-term care had multiple origins, but the lack of any succession planning for Hallman Construction lay at its foundation. Both Peter and Jim had been actively working in and managing key areas of the family business. By the early 1990s, when both had come to the realization that their father was not seriously entertaining any meaningful transfer of control, Jim raised the idea of getting into the retirement home business as "something we should do." However, it was Peter with his wife, Brenda, who first turned this concept into reality by building and opening Bankside Terraces in Kitchener in 1996.

The ownership of the retirement homes took some time to sort out. Financing for the homes originated from their family equity, which Lyle still controlled even though technically it belonged to Peter, Susan, and Jim. Eventually, the entire Terraces by Hallman venture was structured as a next-generation partnership. The Queen's Square retirement home in Cambridge was just opening when Peter died. In 2004, the Guelph retirement home opened up—its construction had begun before Lyle's passing. Looking back, Jim believes that if his father hadn't died so suddenly, he might have expanded and built more retirement homes, since as he said, "We did this well."

Building and managing retirement homes was quite enjoyable for Jim, although it wasn't always easy. After his brother's death, four major challenges immediately presented themselves.

The first major challenge came with the loss of Peter. After his son's death, Lyle had less confidence in the potential of the new venture and asked Jim to arrange alternative financing. Jim was able to accomplish this relatively quickly.

The second major challenge was a need to re-examine existing partnerships. In order to move into the retirement home sector with immediate credibility and experience, Peter had partnered with Riverview Terrace in Brantford. This partnership provided most of the initial operational management savvy and shaped the early culture of their homes. However, Peter and Jim had already discussed their concerns about the long-term viability of the arrangement. Eventually, Jim concluded that the philosophy of the Brantford partners did not align with his own, and the partnership was dissolved so that Hallman Eldercare could move in a direction that more clearly reflected the values and culture of the Hallman family.

The third major challenge was simply the day-to-day management of the retirement homes. Until 1999, Jim had been a passive investor/owner. To help manage and expand the retirement homes, and to nurture the culture of collaboration he desired, Jim reached out to Lyn Fisher. Lyn had originally been hired by Peter in 1998 to manage the Queen's Square retirement home. She recalls Peter as someone who commanded respect and had a distinct vision he was able to translate to the staff—"to give residents the same quality of life as they had before." Peter had a great heart for the business, or as Lyn put it, "He just had a great heart." Lyn remembers that the Hallmans behaved "as if they were taking care of their own mom."

As vice-president of operations at head office, Lyn became fully involved in the collaborative work of writing organizational and staff policies.

"The Hallmans allowed me to practise more of what I believed," she said. "The residents have to see staff happy so they also feel more comfortable." With Jim's encouragement, she nurtured a culture where front-line staff felt valued.

Lyn remains effusive in her praise. "We worked in such a great company. The Hallmans cared not just *for* the residents, but they cared *about* them as well. And that caring began with supportive nurturing of their staff."

Lyn remained with the Hallmans from 1997 to 2007 and had the privilege of working with both Peter (for two years) and Jim. When asked to compare their leadership styles, she echoed what many others have said. Peter was seen as a strong, vibrant corporate leader. He was incredibly self-confident and quite serious around staff. But key managers also recalled his gentle sense of humour. She found him highly intelligent, noting that you really had to work to convince Peter of your point of view, but that he remained an effective and open listener.

Staff members found that Peter invested fully in everything he did at the homes—he always gave his all. He also commanded respect and could be rather intense about maintaining certain standards. Nothing agitated him more than seeing a staff member come into one of his buildings with a Tim Hortons or Starbucks coffee. He considered that a violation of the culture the Hallmans were trying to create.

"Isn't our coffee good enough?" he'd ask.

As operating owner from 1999 to 2007, Jim demonstrated a leadership style that seemed more hands-off, directing all operational decisions to his managers and ultimately his vice-president, Lyn. He was viewed as an effective communicator with an open door. Although it was clear where the line was, Jim was definitely a more relaxed leader. He had a gift for keeping everyone in a happy frame of mind—his leadership style was frequently described as fun and approachable. Staff recall Jim and Sue's exceptional kindness—treating them as well as the residents as family. And it was the combination of these qualities that commanded respect. After the sale of the homes, Lyn continued a very successful career in the industry.

Looking back, she says, "Jim was so much fun to work with; I have never enjoyed myself so much."

The fourth and final challenge proved insurmountable. By the early 2000s, Jim was beginning to truly enjoy running the retirement homes. After Peter's death, he completed another home and seemed poised to assertively expand further into the region and throughout Ontario. He had turned the Hallman Eldercare's retirement homes around financially, streamlining their operations, building up their financial reserves, and developing the management team. The organization had an industry-leading operational leader in Lyn and had successfully shifted the culture to emphasize "taking care of people." For Jim and Sue, making money was not the only bottom line that mattered, and as a result they had earned a strong reputation and profile in the industry. Jim always seemed surprised by how well known the Hallman Eldercare Terraces were.

Why then did they sell the homes in 2007? To this day, Jim regrets that decision and considers it one of the worst business moves he ever made. It was rooted in Lyle's unexpected death in 2003 and the sudden requirement for Jim to once again take on the role of clean-up hitter. As he rebuilt some enterprises and wound down others, he realized that any serious effort would require his full-time attention and a ten- to twenty-five-year commitment. He also knew that if he took the risk and made such a long-term commitment, he wanted to do so by himself, with complete ownership and full, independent authority. Yet that desire was at odds with his efforts at the time to explore the possibility of positioning the business for intergenerational success. In retrospect, it seems that the timing was off.

RELENTLESS PURSUIT OF EXCELLENCE

When Jim Hallman was honoured at the 2018 Kitchener Citizen of the Year event, speaker Cathy Brothers reminisced about his board leadership of Carizon, a leading family and community services agency in Waterloo Region. She had served as CEO of this organization under Jim. Cathy recalled how he had been instrumental in changing the culture of the board and eventually the entire organization. Before his arrival, a perennial debate among board members centred around one question: "When is big, big enough?"

With a twinkle in her eye, Cathy spoke of Jim—the incoming board chair and a man known to be somewhat shy—teaching the entire board to sing a new theme song during their 2005 strategic planning meeting—the theme of Pinky and the Brain, an animated series with oft-quoted lyrics:

"Gee, Brain, what do you wanna do tonight?"

"The same thing we do every night, Pinky. Try to take over the world!"

"…Before each night is done their plan will be unfurled; by the dawning of the sun, they'll take over the world. They're Pinky and the Brain…brain, brain, brain, brain…"[41]

Although Jim was known for maintaining silence unless there was something important to be said, he turned to the entire board with a challenge.

"If we are not growing, we are declining, and any business declining won't be around in the long run."

In response to the board's perennial navel-gazing about growth for growth's sake, Jim asked, "You mean there is no more room to grow or needs to be met?"

From then on, Cathy concluded, "Within its sector, Carizon adopted the attitude of 'trying to take over the world.' We have Jim's leadership to thank for that."

Under Jim's leadership, the agency, which had been known as Catholic Family Counselling, grew to become Carizon, developing partnerships across the entire region, particularly around the issue of family violence. One of his early successes was a $2.5 million project designed to centralize thirteen agencies under one roof to address family violence in Waterloo Region. Previously, victims of violence were forced to travel from agency to agency and often fell between the cracks. Jim took the lead in organizing a fundraiser that generated $1 million in a single day by bringing Bill Clinton in as a guest speaker. Less well known is Jim and Sue's spontaneous offer at the end of the evening to match any donation given that day. That action raised an extra $300,000. Jim and Sue received no recognition for that additional donation, nor did they require any.

Cathy said working with Jim was fun, and even as he radically changed the culture, he did so with style and grace. For Jim, though, it wasn't always easy. He confesses that the years he spent on the Carizon board required the steepest learning curve and development of his leadership skills. One former board member recalled that when Jim initially joined the board, he brought a light-hearted approach, laughed a lot, and kept things moving. But it soon became clear that he had a low threshold for nonsense and always brought a clear, results-oriented pragmatism to board deliberations.

GOOD TO GREAT

Looking back at the 1950s, one could identify Lyle as an early supporter of corporate social responsibility. Kitchener-Waterloo builders were feeling the threat of large corporate developers from outside the community who were competing for land. While motivated by business survival, the K-W builders realized these outside developers had no stake in their community and were not contributing to its ongoing vitality and health; they just wanted to generate as much profit as possible.

"They'd fill in the ponds and cut down trees in order to build their houses, then move on,"[42] Lyle said, demonstrating early environmental sensitivities.

"Ironically," Jim says, "we now spend millions and millions of dollars not filling in ponds and not cutting down trees in our developments."

Some recent projects at Hallman Construction that continue the legacy are construction of two significant urban parks alongside land developments. In the Chicopee neighbourhood of Kitchener, Hallman Construction established Eden Oak Trail Park in 2018 with a donation of more than a million dollars. In April of 2021, Jim announced a $3-million donation from Hallman Construction would go toward building Westwood Park, a community park to be established next to their newest Cambridge development. It will serve 4,000 to 6,000 residents of Westwood Village and the surrounding area.

Sight of newly developing Westwood Park in Cambridge.

Eden Oak Trail Park

Forest Creek Development in South Kitchener,
surrounded by woods, ponds, creeks, and trails.

According to author Jim Collins in *Good to Great: Why Some Companies Make the Leap and Others Don't*, leaders of great companies have "always apportioned credit for the success of the company—to other people, to external factors, and good luck. Never to themselves … demonstrating an unwavering resolve to do whatever must be done to produce the best long-term results."

By the end of 2003, Jim had unofficially assumed the mantle of leadership for the Hallman business family. Yet there were three second-generation Hallmans bound together not only by family ties but also through joint ownership of Hallman Eldercare. And between them, Jim, Susan, and Brenda had ten third-generation children, who were all unmarried and under the age of twenty-five at the time.

Jim, however, had already begun making plans to improve how the family worked together. Not wanting to perpetuate the inability of the previous generation to navigate business family dynamics, he spear-headed annual Hallman Terraces family retreats in 2002 and 2003. The first retreat was held in Grand Bend, a beach town on the soft-sand shores of Lake Huron, in November 2002. All members of the three families received the following invitation from Jim:

> We have many things to be thankful for and we have many possibilities and opportunities. Family businesses do work, but in order to work well we need to plan and be united. We need to keep members of the family well informed and we need to be able to help the next generation be happy and successful in what they choose to do. Most importantly, we want to help the next generation dream and reach the goals that they have set for themselves. We hope that this Family Business Retreat will help all of us achieve these goals.

Three larger agenda items dominated these retreats. The first item was to clarify and share their current thinking on short-haul versus long-haul strategies for the business. At the time, Hallman Eldercare operated three retirement homes in Kitchener, Waterloo, and Cambridge with about

130 employees. The second item centred on the question "Is Terraces really a family business or do we just have three different shareholders?" The third item had to do with Jim, Susan, and Brenda's shared concern that their children have realistic expectations regarding both job opportunities and paths to future ownership at Hallman Eldercare.

The Grand Bend retreat was deemed a success. Everyone who was invited attended—fifteen persons in all—and fully participated. There was a notable amount of intergenerational dialogue and meaningful participation of all the in-laws.

One of the key objectives of the retreat was to communicate the same information at the same time to everyone, and this goal was met. The three owners collaboratively explained the nature of Terraces by Hallman from both a historical and operational perspective. There were competitive games to playfully define criteria and qualifications for jobs and future ownership in a way that put everyone at the same level and allowed people to honestly express their individual goals and values. Everyone who attended came away with greater self-awareness and a recognition of the strengths of individual family members. Particularly evident was the dominance of results-oriented personalities within the Hallman clan, but the gathering also honoured the many family members who felt relationships were paramount.

The retreat led to other benefits as well. A larger realization emerged that the Hallmans at the retreat were clearly a business family of sorts, but not a new family business. It also provided a small-but-important step in the ongoing healing from the loss of Peter, who had been a husband, father, uncle, and in-law to those gathered. Participants were constantly reminded of "our Hallman family values" in ways that were not only talked about but shown in the operation of their business. And these values were obvious in the fair and gentle way the family interacted with each other during the entire weekend.

However, by the second retreat at Hockley Valley, a ski resort, in the fall of 2003, the questions had become sharper and goals began to diverge. Creative options for transitioning ownership to the next generation were explored, but the development of Hallman Eldercare seemed too new for anyone to seriously contemplate any meaningful next-generation transition scenarios.

Regardless of the lack of progress on strategic planning, Jim recalled how important it was for the family members at the retreat to remember the positive legacy of Lyle, openly discuss their individual dreams and goals, and simply get together recreationally.[43]

The Hallman business family retreats clarified three major realities that ultimately contributed to the sale of Hallman Eldercare in 2007. First, the third generation was not educated in, had no work experience in, and showed no professional interest in the eldercare industry. Second, during the early 2000s, the third-generation family members were simply too young to make any longer-term professional and financial commitments. Third, Jim realized that Hallman Eldercare was not really functioning as a family business, but rather, it had three distinct owners.

He approached the other two owners, Brenda and Susan, to explore buying them out. But they were not interested and, instead, ended up purchasing Hallman Eldercare from Jim through a mutually satisfactory agreement.

"I just wanted to be released," Jim says, recalling his feelings at the time. About a year after buying him out, Brenda and Susan ended up selling the retirement homes themselves. Their sale of Hallman Eldercare marked the end of the Hallman foray into retirement homes.

The retirement homes experience provided Jim with a huge growth period in his life. He had had to go into a new industry sector and learn how to make that business successful. Managing the retirement homes had been different from anything else he had ever done; in fact, he had never really had to manage before. Jim internalized how not to micromanage through this management experience, even though it was not what had been modelled to him.

"I did the opposite of how I was raised," he said.

He realized when he took over running the homes, "I had to keep it going, in my own style... that I was the clean-up hitter."

At the time, he just hoped he was doing the right thing. Afterwards, he saw it had given him a lot of confidence.

"Damn it," he remembered thinking, "I can do this."

Trying to figure out staffing and how to turn around an entire institutional culture had proved harder than he thought it would be. But it was extremely rewarding, particularly as their family values of "caring and concern" were modelled in the homes.

Being the top decision maker in three major ventures had taken its toll on Jim. For eight years, he was simultaneously running Hallman Construction, Aberdeen Homes, and the retirement homes. Within a span of a few years, he made his second decision to step away from a major enterprise.

After completing a succession plan with his son, Nathan, for Aberdeen Homes, Jim no longer stayed involved in the day-to-day management of the home-building company he had launched a decade before.

Jim was able to let go because he said, "Enough is enough."

There was another leadership clean-up job on the horizon, and his gut told him it might be a rather difficult one. As one of the executors of his father's estate, Jim was involved in early discussions regarding the Lyle S. Hallman Foundation.

ABERDEEN HOMES

Back in 1995, Jim had launched Aberdeen Homes, his new building company, with full backing from his father and completely outside of the Hallman Construction orbit. Lyle provided support by co-signing and supplying all the necessary guarantees for his son's new venture, and there was an understanding that Aberdeen Homes would be able to purchase building lots from Lyle at decent terms. But Jim was determined not to let his father control his destiny, hence the separate corporate structure. Lyle had originally wanted Jim's home-building venture to exist within Hallman Construction, but Peter had opposed the idea.

Aberdeen began as a 50/50 partnership with Jim Hooton, a former ReMax sales agent. It seemed like an ideal collaboration. Jim Hallman knew construction and freely acknowledged he didn't have a clue about the sales side of the business; his partner had sales expertise and loved cleaning-up job sites. With these complementary strengths and very little financial investment, they set out together. Within a few years, however, differences in goals emerged, and they dissolved their partnership. It was a fair separation, accomplished without acrimony—Jim and Sue still visit the Hootons each year in Florida.

Jim brought Nathan into Aberdeen in 2002 after his son completed an undergraduate degree in urban development. By 2005, Aberdeen was a profitable home builder, averaging ten to fifteen new homes annually. But now Jim had too many things on his plate; something had to give. He was determined to plan and implement a timely succession strategy for Aberdeen Homes.

Jim and Sue transferred Aberdeen to Nathan through a commonly used financial vehicle called an estate freeze. It was a financially advantageous deal for Nathan since it allowed him to purchase the company at a time when its value was quite low. In 2020, fifteen years after that transaction, Jim again resumed control of Aberdeen. Looking back, he realized the original transfer was done hastily and during a very stressful time in his own life. More attention could have been devoted to communicating the assumptions and expectations inherent in such a hand-off.

Jim continues to struggle with the inability to make this intergenerational business transfer work out successfully. Even the best clean-up hitters sometimes strike out.

PRESIDENT OF HALLMAN CONSTRUCTION

When asked what he does at Hallman Construction, Jim often replies, "All I do is write big cheques to the foundation" (the Lyle S. Hallman

Foundation). Those who know him well have come to realize that his apparently flippant responses sometimes contain his most distilled truths.

Of course, there is much more to the story.

After Peter passed away in 1999, Lyle appointed Wendy, his second wife, as president of the company. The early 1990s had taught Jim that working together with so many Hallmans in one office within a complex family business was not something he wanted any part of, and he left to start Aberdeen Homes. Although he gave up any formal role in his father's company, he continued to have significant influence within Hallman Construction as Lyle had given Jim ultimate signing authority when he himself was not available. Other than this signing authority, however, Jim was not a part of the Hallman Construction operating company throughout the late 1990s until the time of Lyle's death.

During the turbulent 1990s, Lyle had approached Jim. "I want you to run Hallman Construction," he said.

Though it had been Jim's childhood goal to work at Hallman Construction, and he had always harboured a desire to run the family business one day, he replied, "No, it's Peter's."

Lyle's answer was quick and sharp. "Peter is never getting Hallman Construction … I want you to run it."

In the end, there was no meaningful succession plan, and the leadership transition did not occur until after Lyle's death in 2003. Jim became president of Hallman Construction, and he continues to occupy that position.

Because there was no meaningful transition, including a carefully laid-out succession plan, it became even more necessary for Jim to step up to the plate as a clean-up hitter.

READING OF THE WILL

During his life, Lyle gave the impression he didn't think his children were capable of running Hallman Construction. Yet when Lyle's will was opened, Jim was designated the president of Hallman Construction. To this day, Jim remains puzzled about why his father did it this way.

"It seems like such a control move … not putting me in charge until after he passed away."

Convinced of his own longevity, Lyle aimed to sell off everything he owned by the time he was one hundred years old—in 2022. Some background on his company is helpful to understanding what "everything" means.

Hallman Construction had evolved over time to become, essentially, three operating entities. One entity continued to carry out the traditional home-building activities. By the 1990s, Hallman Construction had also become a large apartment builder and a significant property management division.

One of the key reasons for Lyle's success has always been his shrewd, strategic land purchases. The original intention was simply to stockpile land to supply building lots for his construction company. Eventually, though, land development became the company's primary activity. This was something that Lyle didn't envision when he received a purchase offer for all of his apartments in 2002. He had always claimed not to be emotionally attached to his buildings. His philosophy said, "It's just stuff… If someone pays you the right price, you sell." And so he sold—for $175 million. It was the largest-ever real-estate transaction in Waterloo Region up to that time.

Lyle was now in possession of a lot of cash as well as the land holdings that remained under the umbrella of Hallman Construction. He had been able to amass a significant land base by the mid-1990s with the help of high inflation and cash flow from his apartments. An example of how Lyle unlocked the value of this land can be seen in the case of Grand River South, a 350-acre property that he bought for $1.7 million. The Lackner Shopping Centre occupied seven of those acres and recently sold for $23 million. Other pieces of the property were similarly sold for development as the opportunity arose.

To someone struggling to purchase their first starter home, these numbers may seem outrageously high. But developing raw land and navigating the development process remains incredibly complex.

As one major developer in Waterloo Region quipped, "It is easier to build a nuclear reactor in Ontario than it is to develop land."

Although Lyle loved to buy and own land, land development as a business was about to become much more sophisticated, and soon it became the central, if not exclusive, focus for Hallman Construction.

This background is relevant to Jim's leadership of Hallman Construction and the Lyle S. Hallman Foundation. The foundation was launched in 2003 with a $43 million bequest made by Lyle in his will. He also set up a structure to direct all future Hallman Construction company profits—including profits from land sales—to the foundation. Through Jim's stewardship of Hallman Construction since then, the foundation has grown to be one of the top ten organizations of its kind in Canada. By the time all remaining properties are sold and Hallman Construction is wound down, the Lyle S. Hallman Foundation anticipates having an endowment over $500 million.

This outcome wasn't just a home run; it was a grand slam. This phenomenal growth took guts, calculated risks, and thick skin. And it required the mobilization of all the leadership skills Jim had accumulated over his lifetime.

When Lyle's will was read in 2003, some things became clearer, but other challenges soon emerged. Lyle had established the basic legal structure for the Lyle S. Hallman Foundation the year before his death, expecting to flesh out the details in subsequent years. His sudden passing prevented this from happening, leaving a rudimentary legal structure on paper without an operational entity or identity.

The Lyle S. Hallman Foundation was legally established as a "charitable trust" and not as a "charitable family foundation." Essentially the foundation now owned Hallman Construction through its trustees. It did not take long for Jim to recognize the complex set of challenges inherent in this arrangement. He quickly realized he had inherited the role of designated clean-up hitter once again.

The stakes could not be higher, but the potential rewards for the community of Waterloo Region were enormous. As president of Hallman Construction, Jim was up for the challenge of his life.

THE LYLE S. HALLMAN FOUNDATION

egally, the Lyle S. Hallman Foundation was set up as a "charitable trust," although the term "foundation" is used throughout this book. A charitable trust is very distinct from a charitable family foundation; it is governed by trustees and not the family. That is a major and fundamental distinction. The three named trustees at the foundation's inception in 2003 were Lyle Hallman; Stan Nahrgang, his long-time accountant; and Steve Cameron, his personal lawyer. After Lyle's passing that same year, Jim Hallman was appointed as the third trustee, replacing Lyle. By 2009, three more independent trustees had joined the foundation: Ron Sills, a former Waterloo Region judge; John English, a former Kitchener-Waterloo member of Parliament; and Vivian Zochowski, a lawyer, community leader, and retired executive from the financial services sector. Jim provided all of the transitional leadership and has chaired the foundation's board of trustees since it began operating in 2005.

Many people are confused when they hear this is not a "family" foundation, since it bears the Hallman name. Some think this structure is an advantage because the foundation is not legally controlled by any individual Hallman family member. But there is potentially also a corresponding disadvantage. How do you keep the spirit of Lyle's vision alive when there are fewer and fewer Hallman family members involved? Sorting out the "vision dilemma" was Jim's first big challenge. How could they bring to life Lyle's real intentions, his true vision, and his values within a charitable granting organization—and should they?

Lyle never imagined that the value of his real estate would become much more than his original gift of about $50 million. During his lifetime, Lyle's notion of philanthropy amounted to disbursing $2 million annually. He had not devoted any time to putting the mechanics of what would soon amount to a much larger foundation in place. But to his credit, and the relief of the next generation, he had at least established a legal entity in the form of a charitable trust.

THE FUNCTION OF TRUSTS

Trusts are one among many available estate planning and business succession tools. At their root, to put it quite simply, trusts are used when you don't trust or have confidence in someone or some future situation.

Within family firms, trusts often serve as stark legal reminders that the senior generation (trustees) controls the next generation (beneficiaries). This might be necessary when members of the next generation are quite young or if there are vulnerable family members in need of fiduciary oversight. But trusts can become a problem when they're used indiscriminately with adult children. Nevertheless and despite that caution, there is a widespread use of trusts in transition planning; they can provide elegant technical solutions to a variety of important challenges. Foremost among these, trusts help to minimize taxes and protect assets from potential creditors. Therefore, they often become the first pathway suggested by legal and accounting professionals.

Lyle naturally received similar counsel on establishing trusts. And like many founders, he proceeded with his succession planning, assuming it was enough to gift his children most of his holdings' future growth by freezing his assets. It was a standard textbook approach. The next generation got the growth of some of the assets, but no pathway for controlling those assets. Strong-willed and competent next-generation family members can interpret this kind of approach as benevolent autocracy.

Although the creation of the foundation had put in place a basic structure, Lyle's sudden passing was a difficult transition for the Hallman children because so much was left unspoken. Lyle had never really discussed with any of his children whether or how they might participate in a legacy that also bore their last name. Jim wasn't even aware that his father had established an official foundation until the will was read. Lyle's philanthropic intentions were not clarified until after his death. And his actions during the 1990s had clearly conveyed the message that he did not consider his children capable of running Hallman Construction.

After Lyle's death, Steve Cameron confirmed that Lyle had instructed him to appoint Jim as a trustee "when I am gone." But the overall leadership transference and all the responsibilities this entailed were never contemplated, discussed, or worked through. It was a blind spot for Lyle. After he passed, Jim was left holding the bag. He stepped up to the plate immediately.

One immediate priority was to make sure everything was done properly so that no tax obligations were overlooked or benefits were missed. Jim also took over running the operations of Hallman Construction. He had remained close to his father, and so he was fairly up to date with all of the projects. But, as he was also aware of his limitations, he trusted his advisors.

The forced leadership succession was accomplished rather seamlessly because of his quick actions. The professional advisors noted at the time that Jim demonstrated the same innate entrepreneurial abilities as his father.

DOING RIGHT BY DAD

An early decision by Jim to hire Catherine Motz to guide the strategic and operational planning process for the new foundation proved immensely beneficial. Catherine had been inside counsel at Mutual Life Insurance and consultant to many community and non-profit organizations. She had also served on the board of the Stratford Festival. She first met Lyle when the two served together on the board of K-W Counselling Services.

Lyle was a founding board member of K-W Counselling Services and had remained on the board for fifty years. For Catherine, this assignment was personal.

"I knew Lyle to some extent within the philanthropic community," she said, "and I respected him."

Lyle had occasionally consulted with her husband, Paul Motz, regarding his views of family foundations, and so Catherine was somewhat aware of his personal stance on matters of philanthropy. When she was approached by Jim, the mandate he gave her was clear and practical. He didn't want to waste unnecessary time and emphasized the vital importance of doing right by Lyle. She began her work, deeply aware that the participants were still grieving their father and wanted to honour his intentions. Yet she was also aware of the fact he had deliberately avoided establishing this entity as a family foundation.

Catherine had three primary objectives: First, to engage in strategic planning for the foundation, which meant determining Lyle's intentions. The call was for real adherence to Lyle's wishes. Second, to engage in basic operational planning on a grants process, which meant determining the parameters of what could and could not be funded. This would require exploring Lyle's value system. And third, to prepare for the hiring of an inaugural executive director. The time frame to complete this task was December 2005, the legal deadline for the foundation to be operating and actively issuing grants.

According to Catherine, the dynamics of those early strategic meetings were "akin to taking an obituary or eulogy and then stretching it wide open." Lyle's children, and the professionals who had served Lyle, were initially quite cautious. Everyone felt the weight and responsibility of those meetings and the challenges they were confronting.

"We have to do right by Dad" was a regular refrain.

They also came to an early realization: "Wow, this fund is large—we can really make an impact."

Catherine was struck by how humbled they were by the awareness that their father, even though he had a lot of money, was committed to using that wealth to help the community. After ten intense sessions informed by the existing trust document, they had made significant progress. A mission statement and a set of core values were drafted. An operational blueprint that included a detailed granting process was established, providing structured meaning to the key elements of the stated mission. An initial statement of "grant eligibility criteria and a processing formula" was developed to help guide the foundation in its decisions to accept or decline funding requests. Deadlines were met.

That initial strategic planning process led by Motz was extremely helpful. It continues to guide the foundation to this day. The Hallman family and appointed trustees started with a bare-bones legal trust document and a brief paragraph outlining Lyle's intentions. By putting flesh on the bones of this amazing project, they codified Lyle's wishes and determined some very important practical next steps.

Jim Hallman is surrounded by students (from left) Cameron Stuehler, 5, Emily McKeown, 6, Kourtney Smith, 6, Nicolas Streppel, 5, and Brodie Becker, 6, during a visit to Preston Public School yesterday to announce the creation of new foundation named after his father, Lyle Hallman.

Jim Hallman launches the Lyle S. Hallman Foundation
at Strong Start Charitable Organization, Cambridge, 2004.

At the end of 2004, the foundation was legally established as a charitable trust with its own licence and number. Though the purposes of the foundation and the intended recipients were a "work-in-progress" at the time of Lyle's death, there were general guidelines that reflected the flavour or spirit of Lyle's giving and only one restriction regarding a cap on donations to Christian institutions.

Starting in 2004, the three trustees committed to a process of strategic and operational planning; Susan and Tom joined in that work. The trustees confirmed that planning needed to continue and would include the hiring of an inaugural executive director who would contribute to ongoing development and play a key role in carrying out the foundation's mission.

Mission Statement 2004

The Lyle S. Hallman Charitable Foundation is a private fund continuing a tradition of giving focused in its home of Waterloo Region supporting health, education and youth initiatives that inspire and grow individual and community potential.[44]

OVERCOMING EARLY CHALLENGES

Jim Hallman started looking for the foundation's inaugural executive director. He asked Hulene Montgomery to apply for the position. Although she was contemplating retirement, Hulene was intrigued with the opportunity. She came from a wide-ranging, successful career, having previously managed international social agencies. As well, she had worked for the United Way, for the University of Waterloo as an advancement director, and for the YWCA as executive director.

When Jim met with her for an initial interview, Hulene indicated she liked launching initiatives and usually remained in a position for only five years or so. She ultimately agreed to a three- to five-year commitment to get the operation up and running.

Hulene was an excellent fit for the foundation, and she and Jim had a very productive relationship during extremely difficult times. Her experiences under Jim's leadership were key to their success in weathering the foundation's start-up challenges.

"I could trust Jim with information that was confidential," Hulene said. "I trusted Jim's judgement. Jim could be decisive, and he was very grounded, full of common sense and very comfortable in his own skin—not trying to be someone he wasn't." She soon realized that people regularly underestimated him, particularly when comparing him to his brother Peter. Within the foundation, Jim quickly established himself as very smart, loyal to his team, and humble to a fault.

Had it not been for Jim, Hulene might not have taken the position, as an early encounter with Lyle had not gone well. She first met Lyle when she was director of the YWCA and appealed to him for help in providing safe, affordable housing for women. He immediately and directly said no. It was during the 1986 to 1989 housing crisis, and Lyle had kept some of his units vacant. Hulene was desperate to find housing for the disadvantaged people, but Lyle's philosophy was "a hand up, not a handout." He didn't share her philosophy and he didn't beat around the bush telling her.

Lyle was extremely frugal. One time, for example, while boating in the Caribbean, he lost his watch. One of the crew members dove for it and after some time was able to retrieve it much to Lyle's great delight since he really valued that watch—it was a very ordinary Timex.

He could also be quite creative. He would go to great lengths to source and gift wrap unusual presents for special occasions. One Christmas, he gave his children boxes of rolled wafers and Life Savers candies. They almost threw these away, not realizing Lyle had rolled hundred-dollar bills in each cookie. He also had a mischievous habit of slipping loonies inside Oreo cookies. One memorable Christmas he made puzzle pieces he tucked into his children's other gifts. When they were assembled, the puzzle pieces depicted a cruise ship on which they would all holiday together for Lyle's seventieth birthday. His children soon learned never to throw anything away that came from their father.

Direct, frugal, and creatively humorous—these were personal attributes that Hulene also identified and valued in Jim's leadership of the foundation.

Her tenure, however, proved to be a bumpy ride. It is remarkable how much programming and sophistication she was able to provide, given the many other challenges she had to deal with. Three of her five years at the foundation were consumed with legal difficulties, due in large part to the complexity of Lyle's will and the trust structures he created to minimize his tax liabilities. A separate trust had been established for his spouse, Wendy, to cover any remaining tax obligations of Lyle Hallman's estate upon her death. The intention was to kick a significant tax obligation down the road.

However, the structure wasn't well understood, and on receiving further advice, Wendy initiated a lawsuit against the Hallman estate in 2007. This lawsuit drew the attention of Ontario's Office of the Public Guardian and Trustee (OPGT). The OPGT provides oversight for all charities in Ontario and has immense power. The tribunal judge in the matter became convinced that the interlocking trustees of both the foundation and Hallman Construction were corrupt and unfit to control both organizations.

A YEAR OF MISTRUST

Ontario's Office of the Public Guardian and Trustee traces its origin back more than 500 years to English Common Law, which gives governments a special responsibility to protect the interests of children and mentally incapable adults, and to oversee charitable organizations. The Lieutenant Governor in Council appoints the public guardian and trustee and supervises the delivery of operations by the OPGT through a staff of over 300 in six offices throughout Ontario.

The Lyle S. Hallman Foundation file landed at the OPGT's Toronto bureau, which proceeded to investigate. To the Hallman family and the foundation's trustees, it appeared that the OPGT had already decided they were guilty and were looking for evidence to corroborate their predetermined judgement. They distrusted the leadership of both the Hallman Foundation and Hallman Construction.

Several items did cause the foundation legal grief. The first had to do with the way the trust agreement was written. The OPGT was uncomfortable with the articulated purposes of the foundation, particularly the lack of clarity around the emphasis on "children's issues."

In his will, Lyle's general guidelines focused on four areas: health initiatives, education initiatives, youth initiatives, and "other" initiatives that could inspire and support the growth of individual and community potential. The spirit and intentions of the foundation needed to be translated into an operational focus and measurable criteria. Was the foundation required to fund all of the priorities listed? Did each priority need to be funded equally? What projects could qualify under the category of "other"?

Hulene sought a legal opinion on the last question. During the early discussions, there were differences among the trustees as well. Jim had a more expansive understanding of what "other" could mean, whereas Steve Cameron pushed for a narrower interpretation based on "what Lyle intended."

The question of focus and parameters for donations remains an ongoing challenge even today as the foundation attempts to stay true to Lyle's vision and intentions while also responding to the changing social needs of Waterloo Region. Such challenges are part and parcel of the evolution of any organization of this kind. Meeting these challenges under pressure from a mistrustful regulatory body put an enormous strain on the board and staff of the foundation.

A second question emerged that proved far more serious. How did Hallman Construction relate to the Lyle S. Hallman Foundation in a legal and functional sense? In one regard, the answer was straightforward. The foundation owns the operating company known as Hallman Construction. All profits from the operating company go to the foundation. And the strategic intent was to develop and sell all of the land owned by Hallman Construction within the next few decades. Yet there was concern about the multiple roles the same people were playing in both organizations. To the OPGT, the potential conflicts of interest were red flags. Their investigators didn't like the optics and were convinced that things were amiss.

To assuage the OPGT's concerns, the tribunal judge eventually ruled that Hallman Construction should be wound up and liquidated immediately. Miller Thompson, Steve Cameron's law firm, also wanted the company to wind down, as did the foundation's lawyers. In other words,

all legal and regulatory entities were advocating strongly for the disso-
lution of Hallman Construction. In what was probably Jim Hallman's
shining moment as a leader, he proceeded to inform them that such a
fire sale was <u>not</u> going to happen. Thus began a three-year battle that
nobody thought he could win.

Sick and tired of having his integrity called into question, Jim stepped
up to the plate and hit a home run. Had he rolled over and accepted
the original ruling by the tribunal judge, the foundation would have
remained a small regional granting organization that was gifting around
$1 to $2 million annually to Waterloo Region at that time, because the
foundation's assets would have been largely capped at the level Lyle had
originally funded. But Jim was convinced—and the trustees agreed with
him—that the foundation could realistically more than triple the value
of its assets over the next twenty years under a more business-like strategic development plan.

So Jim dug in his heels—he has been more than vindicated.

Today, a little more than halfway through those twenty years, the
foundation's assets have grown to more than eight times their original
value, and they are still growing, thanks to Jim's strategic leadership
of Hallman Construction. What this means for Waterloo Region
is incalculable.

Jim hit a grand slam. But the achievement came with significant personal costs. Everyone "lawyered up."

Steve Cameron, Lyle's former attorney and the man who had helped
him set up the charitable trust, found himself under siege by his own law
firm, Miller Thompson, which was not happy with aspects of the final
structure. He had to find personal legal counsel. The foundation had its
own legal representation, but that lawyer didn't trust Jim, convinced he
was co-mingling foundation and corporate funds. PWC, the accounting
firm that had set up the original complex tax structure under scrutiny,
felt it necessary to obtain legal assistance. Even the insurance company
retained legal representation. The remaining trustees, Stan Nahrgang,
and, of course, Jim had to retain legal assistance. It got so bad that even

Susan and Tom eventually sought legal representation. During one lengthy and difficult mediation session, more than ten legal representatives sat around the table, each representing separate interests.

Prolonging the entire ordeal was the fact that the OPGT continued to doubt Jim's explanations, regardless of how many boxes of files and financial records were submitted to them. It was an ugly situation for foundation staff. Both OPGT and foundation lawyers secretly instructed staff to personally deliver banker boxes of particular financial and legal files to their Toronto offices.

The outside lawyers asked Hulene, "Are you sure you can trust the trustees?"

"I am one hundred percent sure I can trust them," she insisted, "or else I would not be working here." The duress they were under also seemed to change after Jim assured them that "You don't have to go around looking for ghosts."

The OPGT finally brought in a private auditor to physically reside at the foundation and monitor its operations for an entire year at a cost to the foundation of over $15,000 each month. This person was assigned to uncover the fraud that the OPGT was convinced was occurring. Ultimately, he completely exonerated the leadership of both the foundation and Hallman Construction.

The auditor soon came to the conclusion that, although the trustees might not have always been very sophisticated, they had always operated and continued to operate with complete integrity. He found no evidence of anything unethical occurring. It became patently obvious to him that the trustees had spent two entire years attempting to honour and implement Lyle's intentions. Two minor transactional issues that had seemed suspicious were unearthed and quickly corrected. One related to a donation that had mistakenly gone out under the wrong name. The other had to do with foundation funds that were inadvertently used to build the office. Neither transaction involved a significant amount of money, and after a thorough forensic investigation, they were simply reversed. In the end, the OPGT gave the foundation a glowing report.

Early in this seven-year ordeal, Jim realized the foundation required more sophistication. He began with structural changes to increase the independence, depth, and diversity of the board by adding three new members. Vivian Zochowski joined the board in 2009 and continues to serve as a trustee. She was a lawyer and a retired senior insurance executive with twenty-six years' experience in estate planning, investments, finance, and capital markets. She had previously served as the board chair for St. Mary's General Hospital, the Kitchener Waterloo Community Foundation, and Carizon Family and Community Services, and had helped deliver the Governance Boot Camp for Boards through Capacity Canada.

The Honourable Ron Sills joined the board as a retired judge. He had been appointed as a judge in 1992 and served in Waterloo for twenty-one years. Later in his career, he presided over the judicial inquiry into the city's RIM Park financing scandal. Ron was an active volunteer in community organizations, including the Canadian Red Cross Society, Big Brothers Big Sisters of KW, the Canadian Junior Chamber of Commerce, the United Way, the Kitchener Waterloo Community Foundation, and St. Mary's General Hospital.

John English joined the foundation as the former Liberal member of Parliament for Kitchener (1993 to 1997). As a writer, he was probably best known for authoring award-winning biographies of former Canadian prime ministers, including a highly acclaimed two-volume biography of Lester B. Pearson and a definitive two-volume biography of Pierre Elliott Trudeau. He also served as the executive director of the Centre for International Governance Innovation and, in 2016, was named an Officer of the Order of Canada.

The foundation had survived the OPGT ordeal, which began with the challenge regarding the independence of trustees. Jim vowed to upgrade the governance of the foundation to reflect its truly independent nature. Adding non-family board members, particularly of the calibre of Vivian Zochowski, Ron Sills, and John English, allowed the foundation to take bigger risks, unfettered by what individual Hallman family members might think.

Jim took pride in the quality and independence of all the trustees. Nobody was there to build a résumé. Even as these additions clearly underlined the fact that it had never been a "family foundation," the new trustees were excited to join the organization because of Jim's active leadership and to continue with Lyle's spirit and vision. There was no conflict between the values of independence and continuity.

The trustees soon realized there was no requirement or obligation for Jim to chair his father's charitable trust. He and Sue had been doing their own philanthropic work in systematic ways with almost complete anonymity. But the new trustees had seen Jim step up to the plate and fight—whether you call it stubbornness or tenacity—for the long-term benefit of his community. They were eager and honoured to join his team.

Reflecting on those early years, the expanded group considered Jim's role and character, how important he was to their decision to join the board, and the qualities that drew them in.

"Although Jim knows what he wants, he doesn't impose his own views. Rather, he will listen to all sides. Jim will never hog the spotlight. He had his own philanthropic background and was somewhat of a knowledge expert. However, he allowed the executive director to be open to new ideas. Jim was able to foster an open-minded board."

"Jim was always pragmatically inclined and could become a little impatient if he felt the discussions were not making a difference. But he didn't come across with any superiority, was understated to a fault, yet completely self-aware and very confident."

One board member expressed Jim's role as board chair with one word: "impactful."

When he received the 2018 Citizen of the Year Award, everyone experienced Jim as humble, upright, and community minded.

The early years were an extremely stressful chapter in the history of the foundation. For Jim personally, it was one of the hardest periods of his life. This sequence of events has never been made public before. But after so many years, the story deserves telling, and its successful conclusion is worth celebrating.

THE FOUNDATION— 2022 AND BEYOND

The Lyle S. Hallman Foundation currently operates within a framework that offers four levels of oversight and accountability. Legally, it is a charitable trust and continues to function under the jurisdiction of the Office of the Public Guardian and Trust. Governance of this trust is provided by the board of trustees, which currently consists of Jim Hallman (chair), Steve Cameron, Vivian Zochowski, Wayne Kemick, Andrea Witzel, and Elizabeth Witmer. The foundation operates with a staff led by Laura Manning, executive director; Abbie Grafstein, manager of grants and community investment; Garry Haack, grants and administration officer; and Emily Van Giessen, administration and logistics coordinator. A voluntary Donations Advisory Council helps staff process applications to the granting program.

Lyle S. Hallman Foundation Staff, 2022. From left to right, Garry Haack, Abbie Grafstein, Emily Van Giessen, Jim Hallman, Laura Manning.

Lyle S. Hallman Foundation Board, 2022. From left to right, (seated) Wayne Kemick, Wayne's service dog, Kieran, Jim Hallman, Andrea Witzel; (standing) Elizabeth Witmer, Vivian Zochowski, Steve Cameron.

Community collaboration has become a hallmark of the Hallman Foundation. Both formally and informally, through collaboration across the private, public, and not-for-profit sectors, the foundation engages with thought leaders, grantees, stakeholders, and other funders to fulfill its mission and address complex challenges. Its partnerships include philanthropic and community-sector networks, such as the Philanthropic Foundations of Canada (member), Imagine Canada (sector champion), the Ontario Nonprofit Network (connector), the Grantmakers for Effective Organizations (member), as well as those focused on change, such as the Waterloo Region Children and Youth Planning Table and the Early Child Development Funders Working Group.

PROGRAMS AND INITIATIVES

The foundation funds programs and initiatives in the following areas:

CHILDREN'S INITIATIVES

Children's initiatives—particularly those targeting the healthy development of children from birth to age twelve—continue to be a funding priority. The foundation prioritizes initiatives that "focus on primary prevention and strategies which promote children's wellness and proactively address potential problems by providing opportunities for learning and growth."[45] The foundation acknowledges and values the vital role played by caregivers, parents, schools, neighbours, and the community at large in raising healthy children. Its vision and funding priorities align with the vision of a community, where every child is supported and encouraged to reach their full potential.

CHILDREN AND YOUTH CAPITAL

The foundation also prioritizes funding capital programs for children and youth. These grants are meant to increase access to facilities offering recreational and character-building programs for children and youth (from birth to age sixteen) who are from low-income families. Funding requests that aim to provide facilities in areas of high need, or involve shared facilities and collaborative approaches, are given higher consideration.

HIGHER EDUCATION

Higher education has always been an important priority for the foundation; it is clear that education contributes to the overall health and well-being of both individuals and the entire community. The foundation continues to support post-secondary education in Waterloo Region through grants to Conestoga College, Wilfrid Laurier University, and the University of Waterloo. Funding initiatives that improve access to higher education for under-represented groups and those involving community partnership are emphasized.

HEALTH CARE

Since robust health care institutions are fundamental to community well-being, the foundation supports health care in Waterloo Region through grants to Cambridge Memorial Hospital, Grand River Hospital, and St. Mary's General Hospital. Over the years, these community investments have included buildings, equipment, training, and professional development, as well as other specific programs.

GRANTING PILOT PROJECTS

In the spirit of proactive community leadership, the foundation also provides grants for pilot projects. Currently, the foundation is piloting two new and highly innovative types of grants. General operating support (GOS) funding was introduced in 2018 and was boosted as a creative response to COVID-19. This grants to trusted, proven, established organizations unrestricted funds for core operational expenses that would exist regardless of specific program activities. These organizations may provide a lot of programs but still be operationally poor because of the conventional cycle of short-term, project-based funding.

Neighbourhood Action Grants (NAGs) are more entrepreneurial in nature, and pilots were launched in 2018. NAGs are small grants of up to $500 intended to help residents take action on things they care about in their immediate neighbourhood—right at the grassroots level. The goals of the NAG program are to give residents including youth a chance to engage in fun projects that make an impact for their neighbourhoods, to help residents create connections with one another and the places they live in, and to help residents develop their leadership skills, encouraging youth leadership in particular.

The onset of COVID-19 in 2020 dramatically accelerated the strategic intent of the board's funding patterns. In 2021, the foundation supported close to forty programs and projects with over $7 million under the banner of Social Impact Grants. The 2021 Social Impact Grants were a dynamic and innovative departure from traditional funding methods. They were proactive—in other words, no application was requested. Furthermore, these grants were unrestricted; recipients were selected based on three guiding principles:

1. Grants were given to organizations whose initiatives align with the Hallman Foundation mission—that is, focusing on support for young children, parents, and families; taking a preventive approach; reflecting and responding to community needs; and being driven by data and learning.

2. Grants went to organizations that were "investing toward equity" and were disproportionately affected by the pandemic.

3. The foundation invested in "changemakers"—organizations that demonstrated creativity and flexibility and were seeking to address root causes.

VISION, MISSION, VALUES

VISION

The vision of the Hallman Foundation is pithy but personal: "Every child is supported by a caring adult."

MISSION

The foundation's mission follows from the vision: "We invest so that children grow up loved and resilient with families that are strong, neighbourhoods that are connected, institutions that are healthy and systems that are creative and dynamic."

VALUES AND GUIDING PRINCIPLES

The foundation's values and guiding principles are profound and have served to keep the organization singularly focused.

1. We put children, families, and communities first.

    - We intervene early and work to prevent problems faced by children before they start.

    - We believe in and enable the dreams, plans, and wisdom of real people living in real communities.

    - We are locally rooted and globally minded. Our home base and primary priority is Waterloo Region, but we are intentionally building relationships and extending our learning beyond these borders. We seek out, listen to, learn from, and walk with those who live and work in the communities we support.

    - We recognize we are in a unique position to make change happen. We use the power and privilege this brings with humility and in the highest interests of children and community.

2. We invest in impact and play the long game.

    - We fund beyond the status quo. Our investments support resident leadership, innovative services, healthy networks, and collaborative efforts that tackle systemic barriers to well-being.

    - We use evidence, expertise, creativity, and participation to imagine and re-think possible futures.

    - We recognize that lasting change takes time and continued investment. We are willing to start without knowing the end product, as long as we understand the end goal.

3. We are shameless about learning and courageous about leading.

    - We are aware of our capacity to influence and deploy it judiciously, thoughtfully, and bravely.

- We are biased to action. Unwilling to be bound by traditional expectations of charity, we test novel ideas, take risks, and learn from failure. We continuously listen, learn, reflect, and adapt.

- We are willing to move beyond our comfort zone. We accept ambiguity, seek and engage with diverse opinions, and participate in clear, frank, and honest dialogue.

FUNDING WITH HUMILITY

"Humility is kind of baked into your DNA."
Cathy Mann, It Doesn't Hurt to Ask! podcast

This unsolicited and rather remarkable quote on humility was made by Cathy Mann, host of *It Doesn't Hurt to Ask!* podcast, a podcast that talks about fund raising, in 2019 while in conversation with Laura Manning, executive director of the Hallman Foundation.[46]

Cathy mentioned that she had done a lot of research on collective impact and the role of philanthropy, and she saw that most of the funders had to approach that role with a lot of humility. The power dynamic between the grantee and the funder is extremely difficult to navigate. The funder has all the power. They write the cheques, determine the criteria for worthy recipients, evaluate the quality of the results, and define what is acceptable. However, research shows that the best long-term impact occurs when that relationship is approached with great humility.

Laura openly acknowledged that, regardless of the funding, the Hallman Foundation owns that inevitable power differential. But the creative and effective journey for the foundation entails not wielding that power with a heavy hand but mitigating it and building on the deep relationships it already has. The deep listening that characterizes the foundation's empathic humility led directly to two of its latest, ongoing experimental funding approaches.

In 2018, the foundation piloted two new styles of granting (at least, new in the sense of being different from what it had previously done). One entailed neighbourhood-level micro-granting in the form of "neighbourhood action grants." The other involved general operating support.

NAGs, very small grants of up to $500, were funnelled through a charitable partner within specific neighbourhoods. They enabled residents to carry out a project they felt would make their neighbourhood a better place to live. Some of the projects funded include a multicultural potluck, community garage sale, presentation with a guest speaker, youth get-together, and decorating project for a youth room in a community centre. All these event-based activities were intended to deepen community relationships and build a sense of social cohesion. These initiatives started around a basic understanding that later became the foundation's tagline:

"Every child is supported by a caring adult"

In creating the new neighbourhood grant, the foundation listened to neighbourhood residents who were part of the design team, who said, "If you have a neighbourhood where people know and care about each other, they will look after each other's kids. You don't have to be that specific about it."

And so, the foundation loosened up the bureaucratic red tape for these micro-projects, trusting that as it helps build neighbourhoods from the ground up, the other stuff will come. The initial pilot involved two projects. By 2022, the foundation will be supporting eight NAGs.

NEIGHBORHOOD ACTION GRANTS

MEGA-FUN DAY

Abbie Grafstein, manager of grants and community investment at the Lyle S. Hallman Foundation, can't stop talking about the impact of Neighbourhood Action Grants. This grassroots approach to community development emerged after the foundation investigated the successful results of earlier micro-granting projects in both Canada and the United States. These were projects that had helped neighbourhoods realize their dreams for the community.

In typical collaborative fashion, the foundation connected with leaders in two of the region's community centres to help co-design the process. The team came up with the following framework for each NAG: Up to $500 would be available for each project. The neighbourhood would define its own project. At least two community members had to serve as the leads on each project. Staff resources would be required for the application process, administration, and coaching functions.

Capacity funds of $7,000 per year were allocated from the foundation for each community organization that chose to apply. The NAGs were designed to reinforce and build up the leadership capacity within residents of the community. More specifically, the goals were to create fun and engaging projects in the neighbourhood, help residents build connections with each other and the places they live in, and support leadership development. All age groups were eligible; however, the emerging sweet spot for applicants seemed to be the youth—some applicants were as young as ten years old.

The very first project was a community yard sale. The participants were extremely excited about what this yard sale could do with a $500 grant. They had booths, a passport, and prizes, and the organizer was thrilled. The following year, she organized a community yard sale without the grant. She now knew how to do it.

After the resounding success of seven projects in two neighbourhoods—Greenwood Chaplin in Cambridge and Courtland Shelley in Kitchener—during the first year, more projects were added in two additional neighbourhoods: Sunnydale in Waterloo and Preston Heights in Cambridge. In this way, the idea was introduced to new coaches, and the grants received more promotion.

During their second year, Abbie recalls, a coach from a supporting agency coming to a meeting,

"I have two ten-year-old girls who want to run a project," they said.

The girls wanted to organize a Mega-Fun Day—essentially a program to keep neighbourhood kids aged eight to twelve in touch with each other over the summer. For the application, their coach guided them through a strategic planning process, drove the kids to get supplies, and helped them fill out consent forms. The coach also helped them come up with a budget for the application. They ran the day in an amazing fashion, and the capacity event became a proud community moment.

Strategic budgeting process for a Neighbourhood Action Grant project.

MEGA-FUN DAY BUDGETING TEMPLATE.

But the real success resided in the leadership building that took place in these two ten-year-olds. The growth in their confidence was palpable and irrepressible:

"I like doing this, I feel empowered."

"I feel like I can do anything."

"I feel this is a dream."

"I don't believe I actually get to do this."

When foundation staff did a post-event debrief with the girls, all they wanted to talk about was the next event. They had noticed that the grant application form had room to list only two leaders, and they wanted more. The feedback from these ten-year-old girls prompted the foundation to modify the application form—a very visible form of empowerment.

As she reflected, Abbie added, "I believe we are developing neighbourhood action leaders for life."

LITTLE FREE GARDEN

Little Free Garden bench.

Another story reflects the variety of projects eligible for NAGs. Projects can take many forms—a one-time event, learning workshop, or legacy project with a more lasting impact. One resident had an idea for a little free garden—like a free lending library but involving plants rather than books. Original plantings and offerings were put out, lots of promotion was carried out on social media, and people connected virtually.

Then a few neighbours got together to create a bench and painted it, placing it prominently on a front lawn in a high-traffic area. A young man down the street got to know the host of the garden, which formed an evolving mentorship connection. Now the coach reports that there are plans for a fall harvest—the project keeps growing. The community-building aspect of this NAG has already been profound and continues.

One of the larger realizations has always been that connected communities provide greater safety for our children. This is reflected in the foundation's mission to have every child supported by a caring adult.

It is also true that nearly all funding organizations are preoccupied with achieving results, which are usually considered more "noteworthy" if they achieve demonstrated, measurable outcomes. This has led most funders to provide "project-based funding." The Hallman Foundation went through a process dubbed "shameless learning" when it began to consider the possibility of providing general operating support. In the past, support for general administrative costs, such as professional development or evaluation, tended to be restricted. Although it was not an easy process, the foundation chose to take the risk of moving beyond project-based funding to offer completely unrestricted operating support to organizations it believed in.

This is tricky territory for many funders. What about the foundation's fiduciary responsibility? What guarantees are there that these organizations would spend the funds in the best interests of the community?

It took the foundation's board some time to become comfortable with these predictable accountability challenges. When board members expressed concerns about money being spent "badly," staff members responded, "Who and what defines badly?" It was a question of trust in the grant recipients.

This approach to funding was a huge departure from anything the foundation had done before. Under Jim's leadership, it was part of the foundation's learning journey, an example of the shameless learning identified as a value of the organization.

The DNA of humility comes right from the top. And it has always involved lots of listening.

CARIZON

Carizon Family and Community Services has been a recipient of funding since the foundation first began its granting program in 2004. The partnership began with one of Carizon's predecessor organizations, Catholic Family Counselling, which rebranded itself as Mosaic Counselling and Family Services and then merged with kidsLINK in 2013. Carizon was born out of that merger soon afterwards. It remains one of the largest providers of mental health services in Waterloo Region.

Tracy Elop, CEO of Carizon since 2016, remembers reaching out to Jim Hallman early in her tenure to become better acquainted with their donor base and share current developments at the organization. She and Jim had a number of conversations during the fall of 2020. After walking Jim through Carizon's planning process and updating him on the strategic direction, Tracy was left with a single dominant impression: "What a down-to-earth person." As they concluded their time together, he made a breezy comment.

"That sounds pretty good," he said. "Sue and I haven't donated to Carizon for a few years, so we are going to donate $20,000 for each of the next three years."

Tracy had to pick her jaw off the floor. "He clearly understood the importance of our work," she recalled. "I didn't ask for the money … and it was so generously given."

She added, "Jim is clearly very strategic, and he must have felt that I was on the right track—that I was worth taking a chance on. He was so very open, not controlling. He trusted me enough to not stipulate what we were to spend it on."

Her comments reflect the spirit and values that guide the foundation's general operating support strategy, which began in 2018.

Jim brings a perspective that goes beyond "What can we afford?" and asks instead, "What can we not afford to do?" When you have a really good idea, somebody will come to fund it, and it might very well be Jim.

In the fall of 2018, Laura Manning called Tracy at Carizon and said, "I want to come down to talk to you about something."

The Hallman Foundation executive director told Tracy about the new GOS program and invited her to apply.

"We have been thinking about the amount," she added, "and so we are going to give Carizon $500,000 per year for three years."

Tracy was completely taken aback. Her organization had been struggling to do some restructuring after 2016 but felt unable to take chances because it lacked the general dollars to support its infrastructure.

"This offer was an incredible amount for us. I immediately cried. It was like this burden was lifted off of me—a burden lifted off my whole management team that had been struggling with the ability to serve the community in ways they felt were important and impactful."

Now for the exciting part. Because the funding was unrestricted, Carizon felt even more motivated to use the funds wisely. The psychology changed from one of obligation to one of maximizing impact. How could the organization build something sustainable? Thanks to the Hallman donation and the thinking it generated, Carizon was incredibly well positioned when COVID-19 hit in 2020. It has been able to hire a top development director, build out its information technology/ information services infrastructure, and put into operation a new human resources and donor management system. The organization was well prepared and able to operate remotely in a truly seamless and productive manner throughout the pandemic.

But it gets even better. Tracy recounts that during the past year, as a response to COVID-19, the foundation made a new five-year commitment of $500,000 annually in unrestricted general operating support. Then she received an email from Laura notifying her that Carizon would also receive another $500,000 for "collaborative mental health supports."

Tracy immediately sent an email back to say, "You just made my day!"

"Check your email," Laura replied. "Your day is getting better."

Tracy read the subsequent email: "The LSHF is providing Carizon another $1M of unrestricted funds for 'Social Impact' programs."

During the pandemic, all bets were off. As leader of one of the largest social service organizations in Waterloo Region, Tracy saw that unanticipated needs constantly arose. Having the foundation's funding gave her organization the ability to do what needed to be done.

"We had a safety net. So when it came to supporting the region's safe isolation units or opening a program for socially isolated seniors, we could just do it and not worry about it. We could be flexible and nimble. And to be effective during this unprecedented and unpredictable pandemic, that is what was required. It took a lot of trust that we would spend these funds wisely. And it took a long-term relationship to engender that level of trust."

Organizations such as Carizon ask, "How is it that the Hallman Foundation can do this?" and then they proceed to answer their own question by sharing an example.

Tracy suggests, "I think they have built within the foundation such a trusting environment and a commitment to ongoing improvement."

She cites an early example when Carizon was given funds for a specific three-year period. Because of start-up difficulties and unexpected delays, the agency didn't manage to spend the allotted amount in the first year and wanted to adjust the program. The Hallman Foundation demonstrated great flexibility, indicating that the most important thing was to see the funds spent in a manner that would make the most impact.

"That is so uncommon," Tracy says, "even from a restrictive giving grant. And it encourages us organizations to spend less foolishly. The Hallman Foundation wants you to learn and grow and change as circumstances change. The net result is that they have built up trust like no other foundation has done."

Even after knowing Jim for some time, Tracy admitted to one other surprising discovery. She had no idea until very recently that Jim raced cars.

"I wouldn't have thought this is what he did in his spare time, that he was a risk taker."

She didn't know that, just before their conversation, Jim had again placed in the top five in a very competitive road race at Mosport—at the tender age of sixty-six. Perhaps it is less about taking risks and more about the relentless pursuit of excellence, just like her leadership of Carizon.

Jim Hallman with Tracy Elop, CEO of Carizon, 2021.

The Hallman Foundation's GOS funding strategy was a completely new and innovative approach for the region's social services sector. Much of the learning came from the United States, where there had already been experiments with massive international GOS projects. The foundation invited guests such as Kathy Reich from the Ford Foundation to speak to the board and digested the best research from the Center for Effective Philanthropy and others. One of the board's initial concerns was a fear of creating dependency after two or three years of this kind of operating support.

What if other funders dropped an agency because of the perception that the Hallman Foundation was taking care of them? Would they be creating more problems for these organizations than they solved?

What they learned from the Ford Foundation's experience, supported by research, was that this kind of support actually attracts more donations because of the solid foundation provided by the GOS funding. The foundation began a three-year pilot with the intention of making this kind of funding sustainable over the long haul. It was not a blank cheque; the foundation still retained its quality-control metrics and continued to rely on the deep relationships that had guided the selection of the first recipients for the trial.

The GOS pilot was launched in 2018, with an aim to strengthen the organizations, not expand their services. The pilot would also help the board learn more about this type of funding so they could determine next steps. Should it continue, and if so, how should it be scaled?

The three initial participants—Carizon, YWCA Cambridge, and Kinbridge Community Association—were selected based on the presence of four factors:

1. A mission that focused on children and families and took a preventive approach

2. Strong existing relationship with the Hallman Foundation

3. Learning orientation

4. Commitment to big-picture collaborative work

The evaluation from this initial group was largely complete before COVID-19 began. It demonstrated that a GOS strategy for trusted, established organizations increased their engagement during such a crisis. Based on the first-year success of the pilot project, three more organizations were invited to join the pilot in fall 2020—Early Literacy Alliance of Waterloo Region, The Resilience Project, and Waterloo Region Family Network.[47]

The Hallman Foundation had very deliberate expectations for GOS funding. It was not meant for program expansion but for strengthening systems leadership, strategic capacity, collaborative and collective work, and organizational capacity to support positive change within communities. Findings from the evaluation validated the endeavour, and feedback from leaders of the participating organizations was overwhelmingly positive.

"When I heard," one CEO said, "I laughed, I cried a little bit, I was in shock… I pinched myself. Then I was ready to kick into gear. Operations are NEVER addressed in grants. Grants support programs, but not the infrastructure to keep them going. Being selected to be part of the pilot validated us. It felt really good to be recognized and given this opportunity."[48]

Although Carizon, YWCA Cambridge, and Kinbridge allocated their funding according to their specific needs, there were common investments in core capacity. These included human resources, leadership development, technology and systems, marketing and communications, fundraising/earned income programs, evaluation and measurement, network development, loan repayment, other operational and administrative costs, and training.

The GOS program resulted in significant early wins. Human resources is an unending challenge. Recruitment and retention of talented, experienced staff is often difficult, and chronically low salaries, high turnover, and the morale cost of covering for vacant positions often undermine organizational capacity. One early win was the ability to invest in staffing and talent development. It was the most frequently mentioned benefit of receiving GOS funding:

"We used to nickel-and-dime key positions within the organization. Now we are hiring people at the top of our grid, people with the right skill set and experience. This has made us able to live our strategic plan."

"Typically, when I apply for a grant and have to justify overhead, I always feel like if I ask for the maximum for overhead, we won't get the grant. I don't know how to justify staff salaries, like having to explain we have to eat at the end of the day; we need medical plans. It's so frustrating that funders don't understand that having benefits for staff is important and that is not overhead. It's life."

"We were able to send staff to a leadership conference. We would never have been able to think about that before. This will have positive impact for our culture."

A second early win was that GOS funding also created breathing space. The leadership teams all described working under tremendous pressure and often suffering staff burnout because of work overload and general anxiety over trying to do too much. There was a palpable decrease in pressure as these executives were given the breathing space to come up for air and refocus their mission.

"We were all running as fast as we could, wearing lots of hats. Having a responsibility to keep staff employed, and meeting their needs, there never was a down time, never a space to breathe. We were asking staff to do things that were outside the work of the job description."

"Our mission is to lift and champion. We're able to do that with people in our programs, but not ourselves. We didn't have the capacity to support our own staff. Now we have the funds and breathing space."

A third early win was the sense of opportunity and confidence that came when oppressive funding restrictions were removed. Rather than expanding operations and infrastructure in a piecemeal, stop-gap manner that led to stressful and marginally effective programs and processes, leaders operated with a renewed sense of confidence and opportunity that made better decisions and design possible.

"GOS gives us the confidence as directors to make the decisions that are needed, and it shows we can be nimble and quick and take action."

"2020 is an apocalypse year for us; all our grants end. What it might have looked like without GOS, I can't even imagine. Before we would have chased money and figured out how to make our program into something that looks like it fits. Instead we are testing out things, doing some trial and error in our programs, to see how new things work and to have our own evidence base of what our strengths and best practices are. We are approaching it all with new confidence and a sense of strategy."

Shared learning was an important strategic goal for the foundation, and it clearly emerged as the lived experience of this first group. The leaders in the group emphasized the benefits of the peer learning circle they participated in. They experienced it as a safe place where they could be vulnerable about the challenges they were facing. They were open about the sense of isolation that often accompanies their role. They saw the learning circle as a unique opportunity for mutual support in the company of leaders who share similar values. All expressed their appreciation of and need for this kind of support.[49]

> "I believe that being place-based
> is the way to genuinely have impact."
> Laura Manning, Executive Director, Lyle S. Hallman Foundation

Laura Manning notes that the longer she serves as executive director of the Hallman Foundation, the more she realizes how fundamental the place-based, localized nature of the foundation is to building "really deep relationships with the organizations with whom we partner. Relationships between funder and grantee deepen in rich ways when you sit at multiple tables together in the same community. Both of the new strategic granting initiatives derive from the confidence the foundation has accumulated by being so focused and place-based in the Waterloo Region."

May 2021 brought a need for a deeper understanding of our community. In light of the discovery of the bodies of 215 children buried on the grounds of the former Kamloops Indian Residential School at Tk'emlúps te Secwepemc First Nation, there is a deep recognition within the foundation that the place we have named Waterloo Region also faces special challenges.

As Laura states, "We acknowledge that we have a lot of work to do as a foundation towards reconciliation with Indigenous communities here on the Haldimand Tract where we live and work."[50]

LET'S DO BETTER

Over the past 100 years and even before that, the Hallmans discovered some very basic truths. People have to live somewhere, and they require shelter in order to survive. However, children and families need so much more than a shelter. They also need a home in order to thrive. For it is the nurturing environment of a home, where every child is supported by a caring adult, that allows each succeeding generation to launch. From building houses to nurturing homes—the continuum between just surviving and thriving can be wide.

Arguably, in its 75-year history, Hallman Construction has facilitated the development of, or actually built, more livable dwellings in Waterloo Region than any other developer. In addition, over the past twenty years, largely through the Hallman Foundation, the family has provided leadership by taking up the challenge to improve and strengthen the social supports for children and families in their community.

While Lyle was well known for amassing a fortune as a builder, developer, and landlord, by the time of his death, he was perhaps best known for the money he gave away. He donated over $15 million to charitable work throughout his lifetime. His philanthropic focus often centred on giving children a leg up.

"I want to help provide them," he said, "with the opportunity to make the right choices in their lives."[51]

Celebrating the 75th anniversary of Hallman Construction in 2021, Jim explained the close relationship of the company and the foundation. "All of the profits generated through my work with Hallman

Construction go directly into the work the foundation is doing across Waterloo Region… creating a supportive community for our friends and neighbours is our priority."

During the early 1990s, funding dried up for many of the support mechanisms addressing mental health in Canadian communities. Governments everywhere began closing mental hospitals. The practice of institutionalizing mental health services had become too costly and too bureaucratic. Governments didn't seem to know how to deal with mental health services outside of the traditional institutional hospital system.

But the needs remained and grew exponentially. The result was that many vulnerable people were simply dumped on the street. Caring citizens of the community were forced to take matters into their own hands. Within Waterloo Region, the House of Friendship and The Working Centre were among the many private not-for-profit organizations that stepped up to respond. Their expanded outreach to fill the massive gap left by government cuts coincided with Jim and Sue's renewed personal commitment to give back to the community. They regularly chose to donate more anonymously, a little more entrepreneurially, and outside of the larger Hallman orbit.

Jim had taken the measure of Joe and Steph Mancini, founders of The Working Centre, at the very first Mayor's Dinner—organized by The Working Centre and then-mayor Dom Cardillo of Kitchener— in the early 1990s. The annual event served as a fundraiser for The Working Centre, a social service agency inspired by the Catholic Worker Movement of the 1930s. Because Jim and Sue's focus had always been local and practical, they became strong supporters.

"We were sold on the Mancinis' story," Jim explained, "which came from their beliefs and teachings and resulted in them doing their life's work. They were serving a segment of society that was not on anyone's radar. And they sort of morphed into our lives." The main impulse guiding their donations seems to have been that "these are really good people doing really good work."

Reflecting on his and Sue's early philanthropy, Jim observes, "Whenever Joe and Steph called, it was not 'Will I give?' but 'How much will I give?'"

Then he adds, wryly, "I still believe that Joe and Steph are my ticket into heaven."

Reflecting on the more systemic issues concerning social determinants for wellness and mental health within Waterloo Region, Jim concluded unequivocally, "It has to do with housing!" His insight raises a somewhat delicate question. Profiting from housing construction on the one hand and donating to support subsidized shelters on the other can seem contradictory.

According to Jim, the housing issue has always been about balance. When he first became involved at Hallman Construction, the company found it could get better interest rates to finance its developments if they included a certain percentage of subsidized units. That was the system at the time, and Lyle and Peter were good at using the rules to maximize the return on their investment. Jim recalls that when Habitat for Humanity came into town, the family really struggled with the question of whether to donate land.

"Why would I put money into housing and then compete with myself?" Lyle asked.

Yet ultimately Habitat for Humanity was the only housing-related program they ended up supporting at that time. Jim feels that supporting the people who are the hardest to house is the least we can do. He also continues to make a distinction between supportive housing and subsidized housing.

Jim and Sue's personal giving patterns demonstrate this commitment to assisting the "hardest to house." Gratitude for their blessings in life and a nuanced understanding of the real needs of their community keep them committed to the many people who don't seem to have much of a chance.

Their giving has been extremely purposeful. Sue is very involved with KidsAbility, an organization that empowers children with special needs to realize their full potential. They have also spearheaded the funding to create Hospitality House, a six-bed non-medical residence with twenty-four-hour support for people experiencing persistent homeless-ness with acute and palliative diagnoses who do not qualify for long-term care facilities. Hospitality House also serves people with complex issues who need short-term medical stabilization and do not have secure/safe housing. Jim and Sue feel that, rather than dying under a bridge, these individuals can receive dignified end-of-life hospice care. Another facility they helped to set up is the Victoria Street Psychiatric Centre for the homeless at The Working Centre.

Jim with Joe and Steph Mancini at the Working Centre's "Hospitality House"

Jim and Sue also realized that the poorest of the poor were not receiv-ing dental care. They engaged a retiring dentist in Hamilton to donate his equipment and helped set up a dental centre. And they supported a House of Friendship project that turned the Anselma House into an addiction centre. Although the Hallman Foundation has also supported these organizations and co-sponsored some of these initiatives, their existence reflects the proactive leadership of Jim and Sue Hallman, and the big hearts that beat within.

"There is a lot in this world I don't get," Jim freely confesses. "This is a very difficult issue. Housing is so emotional … Yet, if we don't deal with the psychosocial issues as well, we are not going to help with lasting solutions. And this is why if we don't help people deal with their emotional issues, they will be on the street forever." Here Jim, the ever-pragmatic businessperson, expresses a fundamental truth. His comments also help explain both his own and the foundation's commitment to the social health and well-being of his community.

It does not take long for Jim to return to the central challenge of housing. For him, it's not just about providing a place to live. It's about the need for supportive housing—a safe place for people to stay with someone watching out for them. Those who need supportive housing usually require a secure shelter for an extended period. This is why Jim has been so committed to the House of Friendship and The Working Centre, which both incorporate housing assistance with mental health support. Their efforts focus on providing "upstream assistance" and wrap-around support dealing with the systemic causes of poverty, mental illness, and homelessness.

Within the Hallman Foundation there is strategic interest in influencing change at higher policy levels. This impulse has led the board to seek connections with larger philanthropic organizations. But the pragmatic wisdom of Jim's leadership keeps the foundation from losing its focus on tangible outcomes. As they mature through their experiences in the philanthropy sector, Jim and the foundation have learned that meaningful change occurs either at the top or the bottom. They tend to partner with and invest heavily in agencies that demonstrate the ability to effect real change and meet real, pragmatic criteria.

The people gathered around the foundation board table have a guiding motto: "Let's do better." As the foundation board embarks on strategy sessions for its next chapter, Jim realizes that a significant piece of the strategic challenge will find its way back onto his desk. Although he does not solely determine the foundation's future, he understands his opinions and responses to key questions carry a great deal of weight. And the perennial succession challenge emerges once again. Who is in the wings to succeed Jim as board chair? Does the next chair need to be a Hallman—Jim is quick to add that this decision is not his to make—and for how long should this foundation continue? Will it operate in perpetuity, or should it have a sunset plan?

Since the Hallman Foundation will find itself administering a finite amount of money once Hallman Construction completes the development of its land holdings, this question is a matter of concern to the board. But Jim keeps asking the more strategic question, "What is the best good?"

His primary concern is to determine where this money can do the most good. He also sometimes asks whether larger one-time grants would have a greater effect. His fear is that the foundation could become just another funding organization. Even his preoccupation with these sorts of questions is an example of his unique leadership style.

"Right now we have a reckless chair," he jokes, "and that allows us to push the boundaries a lot. We can take chances—we aren't beholden to anyone as long as we do it properly." Doing things right and maximizing opportunity are Jim's key drivers. The possibilities seem limitless, and since the foundation is run by the board, he is happy that it's not just "a Jim thing."

Strategically, the board has spent a lot of time looking at national organizations and beyond. This has allowed it to become more innovative. A key example is the current emphasis on building sustainability and capacity in the organizations the foundation funds. Laura Manning notes that this funding for operational support is rather unique in Canada.

When asked why no one else does this, she is quick to respond, "It's because of Jim's leadership. We are free of rules and regulations telling us what to do. It would be entirely different if we had the founder looking over our shoulders all the time."

When Jim was interviewed during the writing of this book, he became quite philosophical about the future. Having established a ten-year window to wind down Hallman Construction, he was spending more time ruminating about the next steps for the foundation. He expressed concern that the foundation was already too big and that he might grow tired of the hassles and stress of decision-making. On the other hand, he expressed these sentiments just after arranging another multimillion-dollar loan to develop a new Hallman Construction project that offered significant potential for the foundation. Pandemic uncertainty aside, Jim seems to relish doing these deals.

"It gets me out of bed in the morning."

He remains torn between a desire to conclude his leadership assignments while he is still in good health and the constant sense of obligation toward his current responsibilities.

"I have always wanted to learn," Jim says in a further reflective moment, "although it has never been that easy for me. Growing up I did not follow a traditional path. School did not do it for me. I learned through doing, by making mistakes, through trial and error. I got mostly educated by observing other people and how things worked for them. I never once dreamed that I would be so consumed with absorbing information. But once free of the traditional academic settings, I set out on a lifetime of continuous learning. By absorbing both the victories and defeats that have come my way, I have been able to build confidence in my decisions and choices. I am content with where I am today."

A lifetime of leadership, often driven by duty, yet continually motivated by his tremendous desire to learn and to grow and to do better.

THE END REFLECTS
THE BEGINNING

f the hundred-year-old spirit of Lyle Hallman were to peek into the lives of his children in 2022, what might he say? The continuity of values inherent in the foundation named after him might be a surprise. The ongoing impact of his foundation would surely delight.

The journey of the Hallman business family—the guiding thread in this intergenerational story—has remained consistent. His father, Anson, tithed religiously, his generosity seemingly boundless even during very difficult times. His life reflected the humble origins and barn-raising philosophy of an agrarian Mennonite culture. Lyle also valued giving, and, as he was able, the donations became more and more substantial. Donating to charity became more than just a duty. Giving back to his community, particularly to the poor and needy, and especially providing children with a "hand up" was how Lyle lived his faith and his values. His contribution during his lifetime was primarily one of "doing well" in order to have the means for also "doing good." And he did a lot of good. There is no question that Lyle was proud of the buildings and the programs that were named after him. Establishing the Lyle S. Hallman Foundation became his crowning achievement.

Peter Hallman added a charismatic leadership component to the story through his contribution to community service. With Peter, the

Hallman legacy morphed into a more overt and ever-present engagement in civic leadership. Doing good for him meant that the social fabric of our community was "doing better"—whether defined by educational standards, health indicators, increased mental health services, or progressive educational opportunities for all. The social fabric of Waterloo Region required more than money. Being effective and achieving results demanded top-quality leadership. Peter Hallman recognized that need and was always more than willing and able to provide such leadership and assistance when it was required.

During the past twenty years, the Hallman legacy in Waterloo Region has largely been defined under Jim Hallman's leadership. He has provided both continuity in the form of civic leadership and increased depth and sophistication through his philanthropic contributions. Jim embodies the DNA of humility and caring that has deep roots in his Mennonite upbringing. He has also supplied a level of entrepreneurial excellence in guiding the foundation from its inception to its current impactful level of community building. Many of the business family challenges that might have waylaid others have been largely resolved by Jim.

At its heart, this is a story about a family with a business who were driven to share their good fortune. They have always been strong, passionate, stubborn, and committed. They experienced hardship and success, overcame tragedy and grief, argued and forgave, and learned to lead with love and caring. We are all a collection of our experiences. The Hallmans' collective experience has had an immense impact on Waterloo Region.

The Lyle S. Hallman Foundation is Lyle's dream, his legacy. It continues to inspire and support extraordinary achievements under Jim's steady guidance. And that is a legacy worth celebrating... and emulating.

APPENDIX A:
HALLMAN LEADERSHIP

ROLES, ACHIEVEMENTS, AWARDS

LYLE HALLMAN 1922–2003

- 1942–1945—RCAF; discharged as sergeant navigator in Mosquito planes
- 1945—Founder of Hallman Construction
- 1946—Member of KW Junior Chamber of Commerce; president, 1952
- 1948—Helped form K-W Homebuilders Association
- 1952–1955—Manager for K-W Industrial Exhibition
- 1954—Secretary-treasurer of Buildevco, a large land-holding company
- 1964–1968—Board of Directors, Conrad Grebel College
- 1968—President of Hallman Property Management Limited
- 1980–1985—Treasurer, National Home Builders Association
- 1983—Awarded the Canada 125 Medal
- 1983—Received Beaver Award by Canadian Home Builders' Association for outstanding contribution to the building industry

- 2000—Founder of Strong Start, which helps children from kindergarten to grade 3 learn to read
- 2001—Received honorary doctor of laws from the University of Waterloo, Health Sciences
- 2001—Received Order of Canada for philanthropy
- 2003—Founder of Lyle Shantz Hallman Foundation

PETER HALLMAN 1950–1999

- Co-founder and president of Hallman Eldercare
- President of Hallman Group of Companies
- Chair of Kitchener Waterloo Community Foundation
- Co-founder and chair of Centre for Family Business
- Chair of United Way of Kitchener-Waterloo
- Board chair of Grand River Hospital Corporation
- Board member of K-W Counselling Services
- Board member of Mennonite Credit Union (now Kindred)
- Board chair of Canadian Mental Health Association Waterloo-Wellington Region
- Chair of Breslau Mennonite Church
- Breslau Recreation Association—"Mr Breslau Sports"
- Founder/sponsor of Waterloo Hallman Twins Senior Men's Fastball Team
- Board member of Economical Life Insurance

JIM HALLMAN 1955–

- Founder and president of Aberdeen Homes
- President of Hallman Eldercare
- President of Hallman Construction

- Chair of Lyle S. Hallman Foundation

- Board member of Centre for Family Business (SW Ontario)

- Board member and chair of Catholic Family Counselling Centre (Carizon)

- Sponsor of Hallman Twins Senior Men's Fastball Team

- Chair of First Mennonite Church

- Coach for Minor Hockey League, Kitchener-Waterloo

- Host committee chair of Waterloo Region's bid for Canada Games

- Four-time host committee of International Softball Congress

- Member of ISC (International Softball Congress) Hall of Fame

- Citizen of the Year 2018, Kitchener-Waterloo

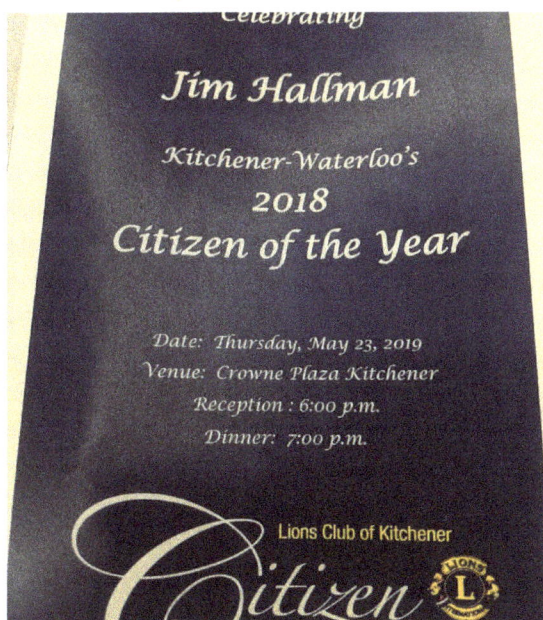

APPENDIX B: LYLE S. HALLMAN FOUNDATION

INVESTMENT VALUES BY DOLLAR

Year	Total investment value
2004	$43,294,055
2005	48,199,589
2006	52,792,963
2007	50,762,072
2008	41,257,233
2009	48,557,161
2010	50,568,539
2011	49.945,718
2012	150,094,731
2013	143,785,505
2014	191,652,548
2015	176,590,020
2016	242,053,697
2017	259,470,601
2018	244,657,257
2019	266,831,235

2020	272,089,198
2021	**321,141,897**
2030	$500,000,000*

* Projected

GRANT PAYMENTS BY YEAR

Year	Grant payments
2004	$6,955,000
2005	3,686,409
2006	2,049,012
2007	2,115,205
2008	469,250
2009	1,282,042
2010	1,451.48
2011	1,662,053
2012	1,794,153
2013	1,686,908
2014	3,957,058
2015	6,863,118
2016	4,471,148
2017	8.371,479
2018	8,159,869
2019	9,530,071
2020	10,119,446
2021	13,985,483
Total	**$88,609,184**

GRANTING TO DATE BY ORGANIZATION

OCTOBER 2021

1. Strong Start Charitable Organization

2. University of Waterloo

3. Carizon Family and Community Services

4. Wilfrid Laurier University

5. Kitchener-Waterloo Counselling Services Incorporated

6. St. Mary's General Hospital Foundation

7. Cambridge Memorial Hospital Foundation

8. Young Women's Christian Association (YWCA) Cambridge

9. KidsAbility Centre for Child Development Foundation

10. Family and Children's Services of the Regional Municipality of Waterloo Foundation

11. Conestoga College Institute of Technology and Advanced Learning

12. House of Friendship

13. Grand River Hospital Foundation

14. Greenway-Chaplin Community Centre

15. Capacity Canada

16. Canadian UNICEF Committee

17. Our Place Family Resource and Early Years Centre

18. THEMUSEUM

19. Kinbridge Community Association

20. Young Men's Christian Association (YMCA) Kitchener-Waterloo

21. Project Read Literacy Network Waterloo-Wellington

22. Waterloo Region Catholic Schools Foundation (WRCSF)

23. Region of Waterloo, Social Services, Children's Services Division

24. The Working Centre

25. Region of Waterloo

26. Kitchener Downtown Community Health Centre

27. Cambridge Self-Help Food Bank

28. Langs Farm Village Association

29. Evergreen

30. Woolwich Community Health Centre

31. Lutherwood

32. Rare Charitable Research Reserve

33. Community Justice Initiatives Waterloo Region

34. Kitchener Waterloo Community Foundation

35. Cambridge and North Dumfries Community Foundation

36. SHORE Centre

37. Waterloo Education Foundation Incorporated

38. St. Paul's University College

39. Waterloo Public Library

40. Kitchener-Waterloo Extend-A-Family Association

41. Muslim Social Services K-W

42. Marillac Place

43. Region of Waterloo Public Health

44. Nutrition for Learning Incorporated

45. Woolwich Recreational Facility Foundation

46. Big Brothers Big Sisters of Waterloo Region

47. Centre for Community Based Research

48. Ray of Hope

49. Corporation of the City of Kitchener

50. Cambridge Shelter Corporation

51. Social Planning Council of Cambridge and North Dumfries

52. Waterloo Region Family Network

53. Philanthropic Foundations Canada

54. Heartwood Place

55. Women's Crisis Services of Waterloo Region (WCSWR)

56. YMCA of Cambridge

57. Mennohomes Incorporated

58. YWCA Kitchener-Waterloo

59. Ontario Coalition for Better Child Care—Child Care Education Ontario Incorporated

60. Region of Waterloo Library

61. KW Symphony

62. Ayr Skatepark Committee Incorporated

63. Community Support Connections

64. Grand River Conservation Foundation

65. Hospice Waterloo Region

66. Kitchener-Waterloo Multicultural Centre Incorporated

67. Future Vision Ministries (Canada)

68. J Steckle Heritage Homestead

69. kidsLINK

70. Kitchener Public Library

71. Southwestern Ontario Youth for Christ

72. Atkinson Centre—Ontario Institute for Studies in Education

73. Big Brothers Big Sisters of Cambridge

74. oneROOF Youth Services

75. United Way of KW and Area

76. Woolwich Counselling Centre

77. Imagine Canada

78. Mennonite Economic Development Associates of Canada/Waterloo Region ASSETS Project

79. Get Active Now—Active Living Resource Centre for Ontarians with a Disability

80. ACCKWA (AIDS Committee of Cambridge, Kitchener, Waterloo, and Area)

81. The Food Bank of Waterloo Region

82. Margaret and Wallace McCain Family Foundation

83. Quest Life Skills Incorporated (doing business as Thrive!)

84. Sanguen Health Centre

85. Opportunities Waterloo Region

86. Preston Heights Community Group

87. Interfaith Community Counselling Centre

88. Central Ayr Playground Rejuvenation Committee c/o Township of North Dumfries

89. Child Witness Centre of Waterloo Region

90. Christian Horizons

91. Mennonite Coalition for Refugee Support

92. Supportive Housing of Waterloo

93. African Family Revival Organization (AFRO)

94. Waterloo Regional Arts Council/Alliance for a Grand Community

95. Planned Lifetime Networks

96. Shalom Counselling Services Waterloo

97. Fiddlesticks Community Centre

98. HopeSpring Cancer Support Centre

99. Anishnabeg Outreach

100. Coalition of Muslim Women KW

101. White Owl Native Ancestry Association

DEDICATION— JIM HALLMAN

There are many people I need to thank for my incredible journey, from past staff at Hallman Construction to people at Aberdeen Homes and the Terraces by Hallman retirement homes, to the many offshoot companies and projects along the way and, finally, everyone at the Hallman Foundation. Advice and encouragement from community friends and fellow business partners has left an enduring mark on my life.

My extended family remains a bedrock of support, continually grounding my decisions within our unique circle of love. Our daughter, Kerri; Jeremy; and grandkids, Tyler and Rachel, continue to bring us immense joy. Our son, Nathan, and family are currently not as active in our life, and we do miss them. My brother Tom and sister, Susan, for always being there, and to Peter for leading the way. Conversations and fellowship I have had with various nieces and nephews is more important to me than they can imagine, and it has kept me humble. Many, many people have played an important role in the story, whether they were aware at the time or not.

Particular thanks goes to John Fast for taking on this writing project and remaining professionally objective, particularly around delicate family dynamics. And for his unwavering assistance when things looked bleakest and my motivation flagged. Paul Grespan has been with me through the many good times and also the tough moments. He has always been there for my family to lean on, and we always knew he had our best interest at heart. And a big thank you for helping to make Hallman Construction what it is today. Both Paul and John remain huge influences in my life, always willing to lend an ear and keep me moving forward.

Although the Hallman legacy as it has been organized and shared in this book is rather male-centric, I want to acknowledge two other hugely important people in my life: my mom, Dorothy, and my wife, Sue.

While Mom did not always have it easy, or make it easy on herself, she was always there for me. Ready to bandage me up or serve treats to the multitude of kids who would gravitate to our backyard while growing up. She has been the one most-constant presence in my life. Whether it was on our various boats or at the cottage at the end of each summer, she was always there providing whatever was needed. She died peacefully early in 2021, and what I miss the most are my impromptu visits to the house she lived in for close to seventy years and sitting in the shade on the front porch, just passing the time in easy conversation. She was a constant reminder to keep an active mind and body, as she lived independently and on her own terms until the age of ninety-seven.

My wife, Sue, and I have been together for many years—meeting in high school and building a life after that. While we married quite young and were not given much hope for a lasting marriage, we are currently celebrating forty-seven committed years together, and counting. Much like the fortitude described within these pages, Sue and I have made it work. We have faced whatever has come our way together; we make a good team. Sue has continually, unfailingly supported me in whatever I have tried to do. It is great to know she has always had my back. This journey has been as much hers as it has been mine.

My thanks finally to my father, Lyle… Dad. Without him, there would be no legacy. I give thanks every day for the advantages and opportunities given to me that have allowed me to finally be able to prove myself. While Dad and I did not always see eye to eye, we were able to put aside our differences most of the time and have a meaningful and enjoyable relationship. For our time together, from the many hours of him taking me to my hockey games, to stock car races, to lots of water passing under the various boat hulls he had over his boating life, to times at his cottage, both during construction and later, on weekends, I am forever grateful. One of Sue's and my favourite memories of Dad is being at his cottage one time, just puttering around Lake Muskoka for the day, no rush, no agenda, nothing but enjoying each other's company, eating ice cream and french fries. It is when these thoughts flood through me that I miss him the most.

For all of you who have been such a meaningful part of my learning journey, I thank you. It is to you that I dedicate this book.

Jim and Sue Hallman walking along the Grand River, which flows through Waterloo Region.

ACKNOWLEDGEMENTS—
JOHN G. FAST

book like this doesn't just magically appear. I want to acknowledge the unwavering support of so many members of the extended Hallman family throughout the compilation and writing of this memoir. They were always open to conversation and provided important materials and encouragement throughout this process. Particular thanks goes to Brenda Hallman and Sue Hallman for providing archival materials as well as their unique perspectives in the drafting of this manuscript.

In many ways, this book ended up being a community collaboration. The Hallman family has had an impact on so many individuals in Waterloo Region, and their friendship circle is vast and loyal. I had absolutely no difficulty finding conversation partners willing to share their perspectives and experiences. This added immeasurable depth to the book. Our conversations were extremely enjoyable, and I wish to apologize in advance for any information I may not have taken in quite accurately. Thank you from the bottom of my heart. At last count, there were over sixty of you who contributed in significant ways by sharing your stories. This is also your book.

Particular and heartfelt appreciation goes to the staff at the Hallman Foundation. As the embodiment of the Hallman legacy in Waterloo

Region, you were sensitive to the fact that this book was not a comprehensive history of your organization, even though the establishment and developing legacy of the foundation figures more prominently as the narrative progresses. Laura Manning, the executive director and public face of this understated-yet-powerful influence in Waterloo Region, provided her unwavering support for this project. Thank you, Garry Haack, for your technical contributions and, Abbie Grafstein, grants manager, for your contagious enthusiasm and for sharing stories of Neighbourhood Action Grants.

A finished manuscript requires much competent assistance to bring it across the finish line. Mark Bachmann provided stellar copyediting and production assistance at various points in this project. Thank you for serving as an invaluable creative conversation partner throughout. I also want to thank FriesenPress Publishing for their utmost professionalism in bringing this manuscript to fruition. Your timely and competent assistance was invaluable.

This book would not have happened without the support and encouragement of Jim Hallman. Jim wanted this book written. He always insisted that the unvarnished story be presented and that you, the readers, would be able to discern the meaningful core. Our collaboration on this manuscript flowed seamlessly because of your generous spirit and your thoughtful thoroughness. Thank you.

ABOUT THE AUTHOR

D r. John Fast is the founding partner and president of Family Enterprise Solutions, a management consulting and training organization that serves family and closely held businesses. After a career teaching at universities in both the United States and Canada, in 1997, John co-founded the Centre for Family Business, affiliated with the University of Waterloo. He has co-authored books and curriculum used by professionals and family firms, including the *Agri-Succession Case Study Commentary*. His 2007 book, *The Family Business Doctor: Ensuring the Long-Term Health of Your Business Family*, continues to help business families meet their unique challenges in hopeful and constructive ways. John is also a founding partner of Power TakeOff, headquartered in Denver and Waterloo, which develops software and data analytics to help organizations achieve energy efficiency.

ENDNOTES

1   "Anthonius A (Heilman) Hallman (abt. 1671–1759)," *WikiTree: The Family Tree*, online genealogy community, https://www.wikitree.com/wiki/Heilman-269.

2   "The will of Anthony Hallman's Will," transcript of Anthony Hallman's will, *The Hallman Family Association*, https://www.hallmanfamilyassociation.com/the-will-of-anthony-hallman.

3   "Benjamin Hallman (1783–1869)," *WikiTree: The Family Tree*, online genealogy community, https://www.wikitree.com/wiki/Hallman-563.

4   Jeff Outhit, "June 28, 1916: Exactly 346 people voted for Berlin to be renamed Kitchener," *The Record*, June 27, 2016, updated April 11, 2020, https://www.therecord.com/news/waterloo-region/2016/06/27/june-28-1916-exactly-346-people-voted-for-berlin-to-be-renamed-kitchener.html.

5   Urie Bender, *The Lyle S. Hallman Story* (Kitchener: Hallman, 1993), 169.

6   Bender, *Hallman*, 28.

7   Bender, *Hallman*, 28.

8   Bender, *Hallman*, 27.

9   Max Weber, *1905, The Protestant Ethic and the Spirit of Capitalism* (New York: Charles Scribner's Sons, 1959).

10   John Wesley, "A Plain Account of Christian Perfection," printed by William Pine, 1766.

11   Menno Simons, "Why I Do Not Cease Teaching and Writing," 1539.

12   Bender, *Hallman*, 35.

13   Bender, *Hallman*, 31.

14   Bender, *Hallman*, 45.

15   Bender, *Hallman*, 53

16   Bender, *Hallman*, 56.

17   Bender, *Hallman*, 59.

18   Bender, *Hallman*, 59.

19   Bender, *Hallman*, 63.

20   "Anne Emma (Hallman) Shantz (1872–1919)," *WikiTree: The Family Tree*, online genealogy community, https://www.wikitree.com/wiki/Hallman-641.

21   Obituary of Douglas Edward Owen, February 2, 2018, Erb and Good Family Funeral Home, https://erbgood.com/tribute/details/13837/Douglas-Owen/obituary.html.

22   Bender, *Hallman*, 81.

23   Christian Aagaard, "An evening to remember Peter Hallman," *KW Record*, April 8, 2000.

24   "Peter Hallman's Community Leadership," The Working Centre Newsletter, April 8, 2000.

25   "In Praise of the Founding Generation," *KW Record*, October 14, 1998.

26   *KW Record*, 1998.

27   *KW Record*, 1998.

28   Bender, *Hallman*, 169.

29   Bender, *Hallman*, 171.

30   The Working Centre Newsletter.

31   "Hallman sells rental Empire," Gotransglobe.com news, June 10, 2003.

32   Del Gingrich, "Hallman, Lyle Shantz (1922–2003)," Global Anabaptist Mennonite Encyclopedia Online, October 2013, https://gameo.org/index.php?title=Hallman,_Lyle_Shantz_(1922-2003).

33   Catherine Motz interview, October 21, 2020.

34   "In Loving Memory, 1999," compiled by Laurence Martin at Breslau Mennonite Church.

35   John Fast, *The Family Business Doctor: Ensuring the Long-Term Health of Your Business Family* (Family Enterprise Solutions, 2007), 110.

36   Briana Hunsberger, "Making a Difference," *Exchange Magazine*, September 2005.

37   Jim Collins, *Good to Great: Why Some Companies Make the Leap … and Others Don't* (New York: HarperBusiness, 2001), 17–40.

38   James Kearney, "The Napkin Manifesto," 2014.

39   Kearney, "Manifesto."

40   ISC Hall of Fame, https://www.iscfastpitch.com/hall-of-fame.

41   "Pinky and the Brain Intro Theme," *YouTube*, https://www.youtube.com/watch?v=qzZmU0aGmcc.

42   Bender, *Hallman*, 75.

43   "Resource for Family Firms," F2, *KW Record*, October 22, 2003.

44   Catherine Motz, consulting and process notes, 2014.

45   The Lyle S. Hallman Foundation, https://www.lshallmanfdn.org/What-we-fund.htm.

46   Cathy Mann, "Episode 13—What if they spend it badly?" *It Doesn't Hurt to Ask!* podcast, with guest Laura Manning, executive director of the Lyle S. Hallman Foundation, https://podbay.fm/p/it-doesnt-hurt-to-ask/e/1569499200.

47   LSHF General Operating Support Pilot Project: Year 1 Evaluation Brief, March 2020, Lyle S. Hallman Foundation, Openly, https://www.lshallmanfdn.org/userContent/documents/GOS_Report-yr1%20public.pdf.

48   LSHF Year 1 Evaluation, 2.

49   LSHF Year 1 Evaluation, 5.

50   LSHF, 2021 Grants Newsletter, 2.

51   "In Praise of the Founding Generation," *KW Record*, October 14, 1998.

READ THE REVIEWS

"How," readers may wonder, "did they let the author say this?" The book's uncommon candor tells a few-holds-barred story showing powerful personalities of common kinship striving together to meet a community's needs.

—*Wally Kroeker*

I am awed by the example of perseverance through some incredible complex, if not only too human family dynamics.

—*Family business member*

It is a must-read epic love story of the Hallman's and their community.

—*Cathy Brothers*

The Hallman Legacy succeeds wonderfully in telling an exceptional family story, while explaining how the business succeeded so well in Waterloo Region, and describing how a good thing, the Foundation, has become a great institution.

—*John English*

This captivating saga weaves a historical account that is better than fiction … a real-world case study that will undoubtedly be dissected in fields of psychology, sociology, and business management.

—*Jake J. Thiessen*

To read this account is to be overwhelmed by how the Hallman's sense of community and civic values shaped their community in ways that few of us could ever have realized. This book will stand the test of time and enrich those who read it.

—*Kenneth McLaughlin*

I am delighted with this important memoir of the Hallmans. They set such an inspiring example during Waterloo's emergence as Canada's leader in innovation. Thus are great institutions and great communities built. Great leaders make a difference. Lyle was one of these giants.

—*The Right Honourable David Johnston*

Empathic while also honestly accurate….a strong narrative providing interesting insight about family dynamics.

—*Karen Redman*

CPSIA information can be obtained
at www.ICGtesting.com
Printed in the USA
BVHW092304061022
648673BV00005B/13

9 781039 143890